WALMART

WALMART
DIARY OF AN ASSOCIATE

HUGO MEUNIER ★ TRANSLATED BY MARY FOSTER

FERNWOOD PUBLISHING
HALIFAX & WINNIPEG

Editing: Jessica Antony
Cover design: Housefires Design & Illustration
Printed and bound in Canada

Originally published in French by Lux Éditeur, Montreal, 2015

Published by Fernwood Publishing
32 Oceanvista Lane, Black Point, Nova Scotia, B0J 1B0
and 748 Broadway Avenue, Winnipeg, Manitoba, R3G 0X3
www.fernwoodpublishing.ca

Fernwood Publishing Company Limited gratefully acknowledges the financial support of the Government of Canada, the Canada Council for the Arts, the Manitoba Department of Culture, Heritage and Tourism under the Manitoba Publishers Marketing Assistance Program and the Province of Manitoba, through the Book Publishing Tax Credit, for our publishing program. We are pleased to work in partnership with the Province of Nova Scotia to develop and promote our creative industries for the benefit of all Nova Scotians.

Canada ❦ Canada Council Conseil des arts NOVA SCOTIA Manitoba
            for the Arts du Canada

Library and Archives Canada Cataloguing in Publication

Title: Walmart : diary of an associate / Hugo Meunier.
Other titles: Walmart. English
Names: Meunier, Hugo, author.
Description: Translation of: Walmart : journal d'un associé. | Includes bibliographical references.
Identifiers: Canadiana (print) 20190046333 | Canadiana (ebook) 20190046376 | ISBN 9781773631325 (softcover) | ISBN 9781773631332 (EPUB) | ISBN 9781773631349 (Kindle)
Subjects: LCSH: Wal-Mart (Firm) | LCSH: Retail trade—Québec (Province)—Montréal—Employees. | LCSH: Discount houses (Retail trade)—Québec (Province)—Montréal—Employees. | LCSH: Working poor—Québec (Province)—Montréal.
Classification: LCC HF5429.215.C3 M4813 2019 | DDC 381/.14906571428—dc23

CONTENTS

*To my family, who supports me in my awk-
ward projects; to the Saint-Léonard
associates; and to Eddie Vedder.*

Kyle: We don't want Wall-Mart in our city.
Receptionist: Who does?
— South Park, "Something Wall-Mart This
Way Comes," Season 8, Episode 9, 2004

There is only one boss. The customer. And he can fire
everybody in the company from the chairman on
down, simply by spending his money somewhere else.
— Sam Walton

★

FOREWORD

"WHAT IF I TRY TO GET HIRED AT WALMART?"

The idea was proposed in a windowless office in the *La Presse* building one day in 2012. Katia, my boss, greeted it with a raised eyebrow. She was no doubt trying to understand what motivates me or was considering whether such a move would generate a story attracting interest. She hesitated. But I was on a roll.

I had just finished a story on a disturbing explosion of youth steroid consumption. I was particularly proud of the title, "*Le secret est dans la sauce* (The Secret is in the Sauce)." The reference was to a 1990s American film, *Fried Green Tomatoes*, in which a wrong-doer is minced up and cooked in a sauce, which the waitresses of a small-town greasy spoon then try to get their customers to swallow (literally). In the world of oversized biceps, sauce refers to steroids, which also carves bodies, though in an entirely different sense.

I like field reporting. I like going out to meet people, especially those we talk a lot about but never bother to really get to know. Lance Armstrong was doping to make millions. Big deal. I leave such mundanities to others. But the kid from Boucherville and the Pointe-Calumet beach club members — why do they shoot steroids? That's less obvious. I want to know. My boss, also excited by field reporting, didn't leave me hanging long. She agreed to the Walmart project; this was not a self-evident decision, because it meant assigning a journalist to a single story for three months. But opportunity makes the thief. Masochists ready to trade the air-conditioned comfort of a newsroom for a minimum-wage job with a non-standard work schedule don't grow on trees.

Immersion journalism is long-haul, thankless work. Weeks of work may produce no story worth publishing. I have nevertheless made it my speciality over the years. I'm in my element; I'm like a fish in water, or a Liberal minister at a fundraising cocktail.

Don't count on me to spot the hot scoop in a report, even if the key information is marked "hot scoop" in multicoloured balloon letters. On the other hand, I have a certain talent for melting into the anonymous masses. Already when I was scribbling for weeklies, I infiltrated a shelter for homeless youth in Laval for several days. Because Laval not only has bungalows, in-ground pools, the horrible Centropolis, corruption and artificial tanning, it also has homeless people.

"An imposter named Mathieu," reads the front page of the *Courrier Laval*.[1] In the photo, I can be seen from the back, hair long and tangled, with a sleeping mat (?!?) under my arm, at the entrance to the centre, which is now closed. Mathieu was the name of my unfortunate made-up persona. I was caught by surprise when the woman at the front desk asked for my name and came up with it in the spot. I then refused to provide the full identity of a friend, the next request. This first experiment in infiltration had certain failings.

I learned the hard way, that very evening, that you can't pass for someone else simply by changing your name and neglecting to comb your hair. In the dormitory I shared with five others — real homeless people — the disguise was soon suspected:

"Hey Mathieu! You aren't a journalist by any chance?" asked my neighbour, as casually as a smoker asks for a light.

"Um, nooo, why?"

"I don't know. You just don't seem like the rest of us."

When I ended up at *La Presse* a few years later, I made a name for myself by infiltrating Justin Trudeau's marriage, and then one of Guy Laliberté's legendary parties on the margins of the Grand Prix. Fortunately, I had refined my immersion techniques, although it might also be easier to pass unnoticed in high society than among the poorest.

Justin and Sophie didn't want their marriage in an Outremont church to become a media spectacle. Justin Trudeau therefore offered an exclusive for his sumptuous wedding to a gossip magazine. "We'll just see about that," my boss of the time may have muttered to himself, just like a bad film, before ordering me to figure out how to attend the private ceremony. My mission: steal a march on the gossip magazine; publish the *entire story* of the pseudo-royal wedding in the following day's edition; secure the triumph of freedom of the press over its censors.

As a new kid on the block, I was unfortunately unable to refuse such an assignment, though the story was light years away from my journalistic ideal. I resigned myself — the Israeli-Palestinian conflict, the famine in Niger, and the war in Iraq would have to wait — and jumped into my car to go rent a gala suit at the nearest tuxedo rental store.

"A suit, no, a tuxedo with a top coat," I asked the clerk, who was only too happy to do quick and easy business. Two hundred bucks later, I barged into the entranceway of the church, just before the wedding march (Mendelssohn's version) started up.

Concealed behind imitation Ray-Bans, I discreetly spied on a species of human that has no idea what "having to tighten your belt" means.

"Your name?" asked a young woman, armed with a guest list and marker.

Think quickly! Think quickly … Extricating my phone from my pocket, I feigned taking a call, brandishing my index finger at the woman's nose as if to say, "give-me-a-second-I-have-an-important-call-I-am-in-the-midst-of-important-business-and-I-don't-have-time-to-mess-around-with-lists-no-doubt-others-do-but-not-me." The woman nodded knowingly to acknowledge that she understood my preoccupation, signalling that she would get back to me later.

In less than two seconds, I was inside the church, my cell phone still glued to my ear. The ceremony was soporific, but my boss was enchanted with the resulting story. Apparently even Justin Trudeau liked it. As legend has it, he actually called the newspaper to ask for a copy of the group photo, taken at the entrance to the church by our photographer, perched on a ladder. He thought it better than the photo by the mandated photographer from the gossip magazine that had been (unsuccessfully) granted a visual exclusive for the wedding. My boss is supposed to have sent him a laminated copy.

Buoyed by the success of this infiltration, I used the cell phone technique again to sneak into a party organized by Guy Laliberté, *Cirque du soleil* top dog, on the occasion of the Formula 1 Grand Prix in Montreal. The excess of this party was surreal. You don't witness the prowess of two stark naked women acrobats every day, with international model Naomi Campbell and race car driver Michael Schumacher chatting next to them as though nothing were happening. I left the party around 11:00 p.m. to speed-write my article before the deadline.

According to my colleague Yves Boisvert, this overly hasty departure was the gaffe of my life; he still believes that leaving Guy Laliberté's very select party before midnight was as absurd as leaving an Eagles concert before hearing "Hotel California." If I had stayed later, with the help of alcohol, I might have seen Naomi Campbell and Michael Schumacher undress and perform their own pirouettes.

Notwithstanding Boisvert's criticism — jealous, no doubt — I built a reputation at the newspaper as an infiltrator. Galvanized by these successes, I next immersed myself in the swingers' milieu with my colleague Anabelle, who played the role of my partner. Under cover as a couple, still in love but determined to break with merciless routine, we gained entry into all sorts of bizarre evenings organized by swingers' clubs in Montreal; including a private house in the suburbs where a cheap version of *Eyes Wide Shut* was performed.

More serious assignments followed: living undercover in a seedy hotel where rooms are booked by the week; rubbing shoulders with farm workers labouring in Quebec's fields; spending a few nights in the shoes of a homeless person in Montreal. Then I got the idea of disguising myself as a Walmart employee to observe, from the inside, the daily life of people earning a living there.

Why Walmart? What more is there to say about this retail giant? The company is no longer viewed as a bogeyman that eats small businesses in their sleep (perhaps because it has already digested all of them); the steamroller of reduced-price fame seems to have avoided controversy for some time now. Everyone loves low prices, it seems; except perhaps those who have enough money to pass them by or your leftist sister-in-law who despises them on principle. Maybe you have gone there yourself, just last week, seduced by the idea of saving a few pennies. Your neighbour, the one who waters his driveway to clear away the little stones, certainly has.

Walmart is much more than a company that sells rebate goods to bargain hunters. The economy is not only a matter of the relationship between merchant and consumer. Between these two stands the worker. The worker is often given little importance. At Walmart, his or her name is withheld; "associate" is the preferred way of referring to him or her.

What does it mean to work for Walmart? What does this enormous company — its workings, its culture — look like when observed from the inside of one of its stores? What is daily life like for those who contribute their time and sweat to the company's success? To live Walmart. To feel it, see it; to rub shoulders with its customers, its bosses; to experience it, physically and psychologically; to witness this reality: this is essentially what motivated my project. When I suggested this field reporting to my boss, I wanted to testify to the experience of the individuals hidden behind the low prices and empty words like "associate."

Why not infiltrate a Burger King or a Canadian Tire? Because the company founded by Sam Walton in Arkansas in the 1960s embodies, more than any other, what work and wealth have become in our current economic system. In the mid-century, General Motors (GM)'s revenues represented about 3 percent of the gross national product (GNP) in the United States; since the 1990s, Walmart's represented 2.5 percent. Walmart is in our era what GM was in the 1950s: the symbol of economic success. But at what cost?

"What is good for the country is good for General Motors and what is good for General Motors is good for the country," maintained Charles Erwin Wilson, GM's big boss, at the beginning of the 1950s. Can as much be said of the America in which Walmart triumphs? It's very far from certain. At least, if we put ourselves in the shoes of the employees. In the 1950s, American capitalism claimed to be better able to improve the conditions of workers than the infamous Soviet Union communist regime, the Cold War enemy. Detroit, nicknamed

Motor City at the time, was an iconic city where the dream of a system allowing — unionized — workers a good standard of living and a fair share of the prosperity was realized. In one generation, the employees of these companies saw their income double.

According to Nelson Lichtenstein and Susan Strasser, Walmart's success marked the end of the domination of the industrial sector of the American economy. These authors explain that, in the nineteenth century, Pennsylvania Railroad was the self-proclaimed standard for the economy. At the beginning of the twentieth century, US Steel played this role, followed mid-century by GM, and now it is clearly Walmart that establishes a new model other businesses are forced to follow if they wish to remain competitive.[2] In their book, *Travailler Plus pour Gagner Moins. La Menace de Walmart* (*Work More to Earn Less. The Threat of Walmart*), Gilles Biassette and Lysiane J. Baudu argue that the "Walmartization" of America consists of a "conversion to an economic model based on importation, distribution, and optimization of logistics chains, more than the industrial and manufacturing excellence that General Motors long symbolized."[3] The new model dictated by Walmart is based on low salaries, few benefits and rapid turn-over of employees because, on the one hand, the company's purchasing power allows it to impose its terms on manufacturers and, on the other, its mastery of global economic flows allows it to impose its discipline on employees. In sum, it is the opposite of the model imposed fifty years earlier by GM, where people landed plum, unionized jobs for life, combined with a good pension and good salaries; benefits that forced even anti-union companies like IBM and Chrysler to conform to the GM model to keep their heads above water. The policy earned GM the nickname Generous Motors. Nowadays, no one would dream of coupling the word "generosity" with the company presently incarnating the direction our economic system is taking.

One glowing, slightly humid fall morning, I took my CV to a Montreal Walmart, in the hope of being hired. Not to pay my rent, because I was still employed by *La Presse* (the total amount I earned during my infiltration, $4,150 net, was later donated to two Montreal organizations[4]), but to gain a little understanding of what it could mean to have to work there to put bread on the table. I was hired. I thus swelled the ranks of this army of more than two million Walmart employees scattered around the world; working undercover at store 3094 in the Saint-Léonard neighbourhood of Montreal for three months.

Here is the story of my incursion into the belly of this retail giant.

CULTURE SHOCK

For months, my colleagues had prepared me for the worst and the worst was today: Boxing Day.

This day is the equivalent of D-Day for the Walmart employee. An hour before opening, a swarm of the strange "bargain-hunter" bug formed outside the store. There were customers as far as the eye could see. As a small concession of mercantilism to the magic of Christmas, the doors only opened in the early afternoon. The associates, however, had been at work since the morning, racing against time to stock the shelves. A special effort was required in the electronics section because each year it was ransacked by customers storming it with a fury worthy of Gengis Khan's hordes. It is not unusual for Boxing Day or Black Friday rushes to turn into virtual riots at Walmart, as numerous youtube videos show.[1]

Waiting for this socially acceptable chaos to kick off, François,[2] the big boss of the store, paced nervously up and down. The pressure seemed to weigh heavily on his shoulders. Preparations had to be perfect.

Two minutes before the opening, our eyes were glued to the doors, against which were squashed the fevered bodies of customers. It made me think of those Garfield suction cups that used to decorate the rear windows of cars, not to mention *The Walking Dead*. The doors opened at last! The customers poured in, some even sprinting. A manager repeated a mantra in a loud, monotone voice, accompanied by a mechanical movement of her arms: "Electronics, this way! Electronics, this way!"

Despite the disorder and rush, the crowd proved docile. It followed the direction indicated into a cordoned-off aisle. The electronics department filled as quickly as a Montreal wading pool during a heatwave. Security agents kept a close watch and controlled access. The store was swarming with shoppers. Barely fifteen minutes after the opening, the first lost child was announced over the intercom. The child had been brought to customer service and its mother was actively sought. It took several more appeals from the intercom before she came to reclaim her progeny.

Until then, Fernando, the kindly greeter, calmed the child by making faces. He was strong, Fernando, and a type unto himself. He was the person who had greeted me three months earlier, the first time I set foot in Walmart store 3094. It was the beginning of my adventure and, while I was as keyed up as the customers on Boxing Day, I didn't share their enthusiasm. I was a little worried, to be honest.

THREE MONTHS EARLIER

A fall drizzle dampened the crowded parking lot. Cars trickled steadily into the mall's two entrances. There was even a traffic jam forming on Langelier Boulevard. cv in hand, I waited in line at the customer service desk. To my left, customers pushed into the store in bunches, like euphoric soldiers breaching a wall.

"Excuse me, ma'am, I would like to work here and I just filled in an application form."

"Only online applications will be considered," declared the lady behind the counter.

False start! I went home to fill in a job application on the company's website. In addition to the usual questions (name, age, professional experience), there was a long questionnaire, a kind of personality test. The gist was, "Are you angry, patient, social, rebellious, and above all docile and malleable?" The theme of informing on colleagues kept cropping up: would you report your colleagues to your superiors if they were guilty of an offence? Even through an anonymous letter? The correct response: yes, in all cases. My loyalty to the company comes before comradery with colleagues, sworn and signed.

My answers to the online form quickly earned me a brief telephone interview with a human resources person. "My advice is to make yourself as available as possible," she told me on the phone, giving me an appointment at the Saint-Léonard store in two days' time.

On the way, I prepared for the one-on-one on which my reporting project depended.

"Go join the others at the back of the store beside the toilets," the clerk at the reception told me this time, realizing from my dynamic and neat appearance (my shirt tucked abnormally into my pants) that I was there for the interview.

The others? What others?

A dozen people were cooling their heels near the washrooms. Mostly teenagers. My future colleagues, if everything went well. Caroline emerged from the end of an aisle in which bedding was piled. Jovial and dynamic, she led us through a maze of stairs and then warehousing. The merchandise stretched as far as the eye could see; piles of boxes mounted to the ceiling, as high as a duplex. We ended up in a room filled with trinkets, tablets, price tags and shelving, nicknamed "the flea market."

A dozen chairs were placed in a semi-circle facing four others, lined up in a row. Caroline disappeared only to return with three other people: two executives and a human resources person. You could have heard a pin drop; you could even have heard it falling. One of the bosses, in a white shirt and black tie, had a bit of fun with our nervousness.

"Are you stressed?" smiled this sturdy fellow, with a grey brush-cut and piercing blue eyes. He was trying to ease the tension. In vain.

The store was to be transformed into a supercentre, meaning that it would soon include a supermarket. There were several positions to fill in the newly opening departments. That was what gave us the pleasure of sitting in this warehouse. The interview would not be banal, Caroline promised us. She had been parachuted into Montreal directly from headquarters in Toronto. We would be here for two hours, she informed us. Two hours! I had thought that fifteen minutes would be sufficient to show I had the necessary skills to work at a Walmart. I had taken this interview very lightly and last night should have followed the *Éduc'alcool* slogan — the one advising that "moderation is always in good taste." The result being that my brain was a little foggy this morning. Big mistake!

The noise of the construction assaulted our ears; particularly mine, rendered hyper-sensitive by last night's excess. Caroline apologized for the din, and then introduced herself — or rather summarized her career with the company. She had worked at Walmart for ten years and had climbed the ladder rung by rung to become the director of human resources.

"Here, the sky is the limit!" she declared confidently. "Who knows, maybe the next president of Walmart is in this room." My misty brain played a trailer in which a young reporter is hired undercover at Walmart, then climbs the ladder rung by rung to become CEO of the multinational. Matt Damon would, for obvious reasons, play my role.

In reality, the next head of the superpower was very unlikely to be seated amongst us at the back of a Montreal warehouse. The current president of Walmart, Doug McMillon, and almost all of its management have MBAS from the most prestigious American schools (diplomas that must have cost the equivalent of at least ten years of a modest Walmart employee's salary).

After introducing herself and extolling the family spirit of the company, Caroline handed us tags with our first names, which we pinned to our clothes. She then distributed a list of questions that each of us was to ask our neighbour. Age, education, dream trip and reason for applying. Once the interviews were finished, the results had to be communicated to the group, "This is Marianne, 16 years old, who is starting her final year of a private secondary school and wants to become a police officer."

Then Marianne extended the courtesy to me, "Hugo Meunier, father of two young children, considerable supermarket experience, isn't afraid of work, a bit of a nomad, and dreams of going to see the pyramids in Egypt."

None of this was false, except the Egyptian fantasy. I have done a lot of travelling but have not yet contracted Nile fever.

Caroline, who had read my cv, asked what had motivated me to leave Western Canada, where I claimed to have spent the past five years. Answer: I believed it was high time to settle down and support my family. The idea of becoming an associate, of having shares in the company and of working with the public appealed to me. The answer was a bit much, but it worked. The bosses nodded happily and scribbled on their tablets. It was in the bag, I could feel it. I would finally overcome the affront of having been rejected by McDonald's while all the other youth my age, even those with IQs barely above volcanic rock, had been hired. Even though I had strategically answered "too perfectionist" to the question "What is your worst fault?" at the interview. This professional defeat remains a total mystery to this day. But let's move on.

Caroline then embarked on a long pep talk, almost as impassioned as Mel Gibson's in *Braveheart*, but at least she didn't have half her face painted blue.

"You will not be working in the bedding, spice or electronics departments. You will be working for Walmart!"

It is true that working in the service of bedding or turnips is unlikely to give rise to vocational fervour. Working for Walmart is more inspiring. I guess. The message was clear: you will find joy in the whole! Future "associates" must contribute to the success of the company, Caroline continued.

"If you don't want to make an effort, to help the company make a profit, stay home. You will only harm the others and everyone's bonus."

It was the first reference to the famous annual bonus, granted each April on the basis of the store's profits for the year.

"Would you prefer to make $200 or $2,000? I prefer $2,000," declared Caroline to tumultuous agreement.

The bonus is the cornerstone of Walmart corporate culture. It's the carrot that leads the employee. We will come back to it.

The important speeches over, we are divided into small groups and handed sheets describing different scenarios, invariably involving a customer. This brave customer is always right, even when he is wrong. He is our employer, he is the one who pays our salary. We must never thwart him, always cater to his whims, sell him what he needs and more. This is not simple. But Caroline knows the tricks of the trade.

You want to sell a cell phone to an older person? Easy! Tell her that her phone will be able to take photos of her grandchildren. Sure sale, she guarantees it. A DVD reader to the mother of a family? She only needs to know one thing: how much it costs and whether it is good quality. Portable radio to a teen? He will probably know more than you about the product but doesn't have money, so he'll hesitate over the price.

Seated on my plastic chair, I wondered what bothered me the most. The totally stupid and infantilizing sales strategies or the certainty that they were effective.

The interview wrapped up. It was time. We all signed a form authorizing a criminal record check to make sure our record was clean. One of the bosses left the room with half of the candidates. Only six of us remained.

"You are here because you stood out," Caroline pronounced.

The elect rejoiced. I was relieved as well, especially since I had thought that the "hiring" part of my reporting would be a mere formality.

We were promised a phone call in the next days if all went well.

HIRED

My CV necessarily contained false information, but much of it was true as well. Because I couldn't admit to my work at *La Presse*, I had to invent an occupation to cover the previous five years and provide references for it. I gave my girlfriend's and brother's phone numbers. The latter had to impersonate my former boss at a hotel in Canmore, in Western Canada, where I had spent the last five years. It was an audacious casting because he speaks English about as well as former Quebec premier Pauline Marois does. My girlfriend had to pretend to be my manager at the supermarket Provigo, where I really had worked for five years while studying. My "former employers" were contacted within two days. Punctual, dynamic, never sick: we would take him back in a flash, they said.

They called me the same day to give me an appointment at the store. It was in the bag. I was an associate! I swelled the ranks of an army of 2.1 million employees in twenty-seven countries around the world, almost one half in the United States. If Walmart were a military power, it would form the second biggest army after China. Thank God I was not joining a light infantry brigade. Instead, I was hired for dairy products.

My salary: $11.05 per hour. I was offered a $1.00 "signing bonus," justified by my vast experience in food. Twenty cents per year of work in a suburban supermarket. The base salary for an associate was $10.05, minimum wage. This meant a fluctuating annual income of about $18,000. A mere pittance.

So little that in 2013, a Cleveland store solicited customers to help its employees before a holiday. "Please Donate Food Items Here, so Associates in Need Can Enjoy Thanksgiving Dinner" was to be read on posters around the store.

"That Walmart would have the audacity to ask low-wage workers to donate food to other low-wage workers — to me, it is a moral outrage," raged a customer in the *Cleveland Plain Dealer*, the daily that exposed the affair.[3]

According to another version of the story, it was the employees who were asked to donate foodstuffs, not customers. A company spokesperson defended this incestuous food drive, arguing with a straight face that it should be seen as a sign of solidarity. The great majority of American associates earned less than $25,000 in 2013. In the same year, the company registered net profits of $17 billion. Obviously, charity begins at home.

According to Gilles Biassette and Lysiane J. Baudu, the income of 60 percent of Walmart's employees is below the poverty line. "While Henry Ford paid his employees well so they could afford to buy his cars," these authors explain, "Walmart pays its employees badly so they are forced to buy its products."[4] The biggest private employee in the world no longer produces members of the middle class, but rather poor workers.

The contrast with the Walton family is obscene. The fortune of the six heirs in 2007 was equivalent to the total income of 30 percent of the least well-off American families.[5]

This gap sometimes creates waves. In August 2013, more than fifty company employees, joined by activists, were arrested by riot police during a sit-in in downtown Los Angeles. The demonstrators had a single demand: all Walmart employees should earn more than $25,000 per year. Fortunately, there is hope because, at Walmart, "the sky is the limit," as Caroline explained to us. All you have to do is climb the ladder to get out of the hole. Once you reach the summit, paying the grocery bill is no longer a problem. H. Lee Scott, Walmart's boss in 2003, earned more than 1500 times the salary of an ordinary, full-time employee. In 2012, Mike Duke, in the same position, had a salary of almost $18 million.

Everything comes in due time to those who wait; conquering without peril, we triumph without glory, as they say. First, I had to prove myself. Starting at the bottom of the heap, in dairy products. For this work, Walmart equipped me with a vest in the store colours. I had to procure, at my own expense, black pants and a white or black t-shirt to complete the uniform. "We have those in the store," a human resources person told me. Before leaving Walmart, I went to the clothing department. One pair of pants and two black t-shirts with the George insignia, Walmart's house brand.

Total cost: $30. Three hours of work.

HEY, I JUST MET YOU ... AND THIS IS CRAZY

Thursday, October 4, 2012, 7:45 a.m.

Today is my father's sixty-third birthday and I am driving like crazy towards the store for my first shift. I have lost the habit of keeping to a fixed schedule. At the newspaper, no one watches my hours. I burn a red light; it would be stupid to arrive late the first day. I park my car in the still empty lot and head for the door.

My life at Walmart had begun.

The human resources associate who met me wasn't sure where to send me. They had hired me for the food section, but significant renovations were underway and the section was upside down. "No access" was written in large letters on the metal fences closing the area off. In any case, I was given a locker and the combination for its lock. Just like in high school. In fact, the entire break room reminded me of high school: a long wall of lockers, several tables with free newspapers lying around everywhere. No windows. And an infernal cacophony of circular saws and hammers. Some employees were having breakfast. Some were concentrating on crossword puzzles. Two others were discussing what they would do if a thief pulled a gun on them. One of them described having lived through that at a corner store.

Just before 8:00 a.m., the associates lined up in front of the electronic time stamp activated by a magnetic card that also served as an identification card. In the staircase to the store, an unavoidable, giant poster reminded us of the associate's golden rule: "The most important person you will speak to today is your next customer." One thing surprised me. We hadn't yet experienced the famous pep talk before starting work. Was it a myth?

I broke the ice in the bedding department. I played fair by confessing my incompetence to the human resources person. No problem. No experience in textiles was required to carry out my task, because I was asked to do 'facing'; that is, placing products on the edge of the shelves to give the illusion that they are well-filled. This is common practice in all supermarkets. I was on home turf, having spent hours doing this in my previous life as a grocery clerk.

In the middle of the store, counters for frozen goods and dairy products were being installed. The symbolic reopening of the store, metamorphized into a supercenter, was just two weeks away. Conversions of this kind were taking place across the continent, to meet the increasingly fierce competition from Target and Costco, as well as the threat represented by other types of businesses that had adapted to Walmart practices. Loblaws, for example, now offers its clientele a line of clothing; Pharmaprix/Shopper's Drug Mart sells food; and big hardware chains like Réno-Dépôt/Home Depot sell toilet paper and candy at the entrance to their stores. Not to mention Dollarama, quietly building an empire by capitalizing on trinkets sold for one, two or three dollars. From about two hundred stores at the beginning of the 2000s, there are now more than eight hundred. Despite the increased number of players in the market, Walmart has maintained growth — but not without a battle.

The company thus invested $500 million into converting thirty-five Canadian stores into "supercenters." There are now 395 stores in Canada; 282 of these are supercenters. In the United States, supercenters have been a fixture for some time. Walmart, favoured by a market fragmentation with great variation from state to state, has also succeeded in becoming the number one food store for Americans. In Canada, conquest of the food sector could prove more difficult because it already has very efficient big players. Metro, Loblaws and Sobey's each hold about 30 percent of this market. Others, like Walmart and Costco, which are soaring, share the rest.

Walmart aims to convert all its stores into supercenters, even though the sale of food is not the most lucrative of its activities. The multinational doesn't even aspire to wipe the big players like Metro and Loblaws off the map, explained Marie-Eve Fournier, a journalist at *La Presse* who has covered Walmart for years. It is simply seeking to strengthen customer loyalty, discouraging them from going elsewhere by getting them used to finding everything at the same location. Once the Saint-Léonard store is converted into a supercenter, customers can do their grocery shopping and find clothes, furniture, pharmaceuticals, shoes, toys, books, televisions, video game consoles and sports goods there. And if they get hungry, they can take a break at McDonald's — whose endlessly repeated ads over the intercom are enough to drive you to murder. In a honeyed, exaggeratedly smiling voice, "Come savour [I hate this word] a delicious coffee or a good hamburger [pronounced ham-beurre-gueure] before, during, or after your shopping!"

The famous fast-food chain's presence in Canadian Walmart stores results from an agreement signed in 1994 between these two capitalist superpowers. There are now 314 McDonald's in Canadian Walmarts. The continual ad in the Saint-Léonard store got on my nerves, but it must have hit the mark because our small outlet was under perpetual siege by customers, who could be seen lined up at the cash at all times of day. Even we employees might easily spend ten minutes of our fifteen-minute break lined up to order a coffee, which we would then have to drink in three minutes. The tables at the back were occupied all day long by a dozen elderly Portuguese men. The Saint-Léonard Walmart McDonald's was their social club.

"I have been here almost ten years and to my knowledge they have always been there," an employee told me.

The customers immediately appear to me to be disadvantaged; unsurprisingly, because the east-end neighbhourhood where my store is located is not the most affluent in Montreal. Its roughly 69,000 residents are less educated and the average annual income of individuals ($24,105) is significantly lower than that of the island as a whole ($28,258). Walmart usually targets less wealthy neighbourhoods and more modest areas and cities, far from the big urban centres. The magic of low prices works better in these areas than in Westmount or

Beverley Hills. Walmart finds both profit and virtue in this; according to the corporation, it lends a helping hand to families who struggle to make ends meet at the end of the month. The bargains, it argues, "save American consumers 10 billion dollars every year, about $600 per year for the average family."[1] Françoise David[2] and protesters of the 2012 Quebec student uprising, take note! You are not the only ones fighting for social justice.

Are products really cheaper at Walmart? According to journalist Marie-Eve Fournier, they are. But only a well-defined range of items such as diapers and laundry soap. Walmart tailors its sales to the needs of its typical customers: young, low-income families.

The clientele at the Saint-Léonard store may not be wealthy, but it is quite amazing. A broad array of characters is to be encountered there: blind people, elderly people in wheelchairs, bent old people hanging onto their shopping carts as though they are walkers, people talking to themselves, people in a hurry, others much less so, numerous mothers with their broods, Haitians, Arabs, Latinos, Italians and of course the old Portuguese fixtures who like the smell of Big Macs. Almost as many anglophones as francophones, hence the need to be bilingual to work in this store. Customers who don't speak either official language make themselves understood through gestures.

I speak English but I am not acquainted with all the secrets of bedding. The mere thought of folding a fitted sheet terrifies me. I thus redirected all my first customers to my colleagues, whose average age was around 60. It was my first day of work and everything was new to me, but one thing I found startling: the large number of open or torn boxes on the shelves; some half-full, others empty. I took the initiative of removing the damaged packages from the shelves and putting them in a cart to bring them to the waste office.

The bedding manager reined me in, "Don't bother with that or the work will never stop," she warned.

The directive was to repair the packaging with tape instead. It took me just a few hours to understand why. Customers had an odd habit of opening packages to check the merchandise before buying it. The practice was prohibited, but the customer, who is always right, didn't bother with such rules. One strange person went so far as to pour out some creamy ceasar salad dressing — probably into another container — before dumping the half-empty plastic bottle back on the shelf.

There were more surprises. A young woman came up to ask, very seriously, if the five-by-eight-foot patterned carpet on sale for $30 would look nice in her dining room.

"Difficult to help you, madame, as I have never been to your place," I candidly replied.

The lady didn't listen, instead asking several times which colour would go best with her oval table.

"I really should unroll one of them!" she finally cried, in a quasi-trance.

Without waiting for my answer, she seized a carpet, ripped off the packaging with the enthusiasm of a child recognizing Lego through wrapping paper, handed one end to me and backed down the aisle to unroll it.

I was a new and vulnerable employee. It was clearly written on my forehead for all to see. My colleagues smiled at the look of confusion on my face. They walked up to us. One of them, tongue in cheek, advised me not to get involved in the lady's machinations.

"I don't want to, but the woman is refusing to listen to me," I told him, desperately.

He laughed and then added, sighing, "It's normal. Customers always take us for a ride."

Great.

At noon, the employees' break room was crowded. Those who were not eating were tapping away on their devices. Ronald McDonald's specialities were popular in the room. Their inimitable odour assaulted my nostrils relentlessly.

I needed air.

I went to eat alone in my car, asking myself what kind of nightmare I gotten myself into this time.

★

In the course of the day, we were summoned to an improvised meeting room in a corner of the warehouse. There were around thirty uncomfortable plastic chairs. The agenda: a workshop on food health with a PowerPoint presentation projected onto the wall. Our presenter headed up food safety for the company in the east of the country.

The written part of the presentation constituted a serious attack on the rules of spelling, but our orator was eloquent. This helped us survive the imposed ordeal, which, to be honest, was useful in numerous ways. "How to identify the presence of rats and other vermin"; "the importance of keeping a log of refrigerator temperatures"; "how are sicknesses such as E coli, flesh-eating bacteria and listeriosis contracted?" All together, we mimed washing our hands at an imaginary sink for twenty seconds; enough time to feel that twenty seconds of hand-rubbing is interminable.

During the break, I fraternized with Mélissa, another recruit. In the time it took to smoke a cigarette, she explained what had brought her here. A single mother who had been on welfare since the birth of her daughter, now five years old, she decided she needed meaning in her life, for herself and her daughter.

"Time passes slowly when you are on welfare," she told me.

She was hired the same day I was and assigned to the meat section, though she had no experience in the area. The company increased her salary by 20 cents per year of maternity because being a stay-at-home mother is a full-time job.

The hygiene training lasted four long hours. Four hours of having Walmart's Food Safety High Five drummed into us.

> Be Clean, Be Healthy
> Keep it Cold, Keep it Hot
> Don't Cross Contaminate (no raw over cooked)
> Wash, Rinse, & Sanitize
> Cook it & Chill it.

The rules were essential, our presenter reminded us.

"In the United States, customers are increasingly turning towards the legal system to denounce problems of insalubrity," he warned in conclusion.

Human persons fear microbes; corporations fear judges.

END OF MY FIRST SHIFT

Richard, one of the bosses, asked me to go see Fernando at the reception for the meeting.

Would it be *the* famous pep talk at last?

Fernando, 60 years old, spends his days on his feet at the front door to greet customers with his nicest smile. That is the essence of his job. There is a Fernando in all Walmart stores around the world. It was founder Sam Walton's brainchild to pay someone to welcome customers. This "aggressive hospitality," to use Walton's term, while artificial, adds a human dimension to the store. The greeter's tasks are described on the company's website under job offers. The greeters smile and warmly welcome customers entering Walmart. They keep the entrance to the store clean. Greeters earn between minimum wage and $11.00 per hour. In America, everything has a price, even good manners.

When I came up to Fernando, he was turning on the radio to play a song throughout store. The same one that had played yesterday and would play again the next day, an unbearable sentimental song for teens sung by a young starlet in vogue whose existence you will doubtlessly forget as soon as you read these lines.

> "Hey, I just met you
> And this is crazy
> But here's my number
> So call me maybe"

Fernando led me back to the bedding department, which had just been revamped; not for the famous pep talk, but for an inauguration. Two pink ribbons ran the length of the aisle and at the end a camera awaited to immortalize the moment. On a table set up for the occasion were house-brand Great Choice cookies set out on Styrofoam plates. Same for the cartons of juice, served at room temperature. There was very little to say about the pillowcases and the fitted sheets. The manager, a rather kind blonde woman, therefore did not inaugurate the aisle with a grandiloquent speech. Instead she summarized the sales figures from the day before and compared them to those of the same day the previous year. A strange exercise, because October 5, 2012 did not fall on the same day of the week as October 5, 2011. It was like comparing apples and oranges. However, the exercise is repeated every day in all stores around the world. Hardware: up $200 (applause); food: up $1,200 (greater applause); and so on. It whips up the troops.

After she reviewed the revenues for each department, the young boss officially opened the bedding section and congratulated the person who had assumed responsibility for it, Gaétanne. Visibly ill-at-ease, the latter hastened to share the glory of the opening with Ginette, a night worker in her sixties with shaved hair and a face betraying a difficult life. Gaétanne softly cut the ribbon. The employees applauded without enthusiasm.

During the break, I ran into Mélissa, puffing on a cigarette. She was worried. She had been told that if she ever messed up a meat delivery, her job would be on the line.

"I wanted to work in fruit and vegetables. I don't want to get thrown out."

For my part, I had been reassigned to setting up the future frozen goods and dairy section. I met my new fellows, including Christian, a man in his early thirties with a hard face, shaved head and tattoos, employed by the company for four years. Difficult to approach, solitary; the kind of guy who liked to be left the hell alone. He talked to me about the annual bonus. The associates seemed to live for it. Christian was confident he would get a good bonus this year. A simple glance at the carts bumper-to-bumper in the aisles was enough to see that the store was making money. Last year, Christian got $1,200. He isn't asking for more. He does his hours. He does his time.

Time for another of my new frozen goods colleagues, Liam, to introduce himself.

"I guess no one has told you anything and you have been left to yourself!" exclaimed the student, who worked part time.

Quite the bloodhound, Liam. "If you have any questions, come see me," he added, before turning on his heel.

I spent the end of my shift dreaming feverishly of the long weekend, which I planned to spend in a cottage in the Eastern Townships with family and friends. I felt an irrepressible desire to drink deeply to absorb the shock of my new life. Caroline called me as I prepared to leave for this dream weekend.

"Hugo, you are coming in on Sunday for a training."

Her tone was final. My crazy desire to drink to immoderation evaporated faster than you could say "bottoms up."

BETWEEN THE ARMY
AND WALT DISNEY

The alarm clock made me jump. It would have woken the dead, but everyone in the cottage was still sleeping, even the children, who had gone to bed late. Dawn had started but the sun, like me, was having a hard time getting up. I donned my associate's uniform in the gloom and tiptoed outside. A dry wind greeted me like a slap in the face. The car was covered with a fine layer of frost I had to scrape off. Steam was coming out of my nostrils.

This didn't surprise me: I was seething with anger.

I was about a two-hour drive away from the store. I silently cursed this mysterious training, and the entire idiotic story. Where does this silly mania for embarking on such arduous projects come from? I graduated in French literature, I could have been a theatre critic. Seems like a carefree career, being a theatre critic. It must be enjoyable to blast a play like Wajdi Mouawad's unbearable lyric lament in his 1998 massacre of Oedipus Rex. As my friends in the cottage were slowly waking up, sipping their lattés, I neared the store and my mysterious training and vented my frustration, entirely gratuitously, at the world of theatre. Better resign myself: I would miss this cozy family Sunday.

As soon as I got there, I found about thirty new associates chatting, crowded into a new improvised meeting room in a corner of the warehouse, though not the same corner as the one used for the hiring interview. Maybe they were trying to send us a message. Like: at Walmart, we don't cut corners in our work. I will face God's judgement for such puns, I know. The tables were arranged in a circle. Caroline was there, this time flanked by Jasmin, a dynamic young executive, responsible among other things for health and safety at work. Carefully ironed white shirt, imposing build, prematurely bald head, trendy glasses; the young man already had a long track record with the company. He announced the day's agenda. Our training was a so-called orientation day — a sort of Walmart 101 — consisting of a complete review of workplace health and safety rules.

Jasmin first explained the importance of group warm-ups at the beginning of each shift. This ritual was as fundamental as the famous pep talk, which turned out not to be a myth and to be based on the same principle as the stretches: rally the troops, create a feeling of belonging. Sam Walton had the idea after visiting a Korean factory in 1975. Asia not only supplies Walmart with soap and electronics, it also lent it its group spirit and iron discipline. Only, in the land of America, all of this became rather grotesque.

Jasmin ordered us to stand up and get started by stretching our necks, then wrists, arms and legs, *alouette*!

Once we were well stretched, Jasmin barked:

"Give me a W!

Give me an A!

Give me an L!"

(… you get the picture)

"What does that make?"

"WALMART" (My lips formed the words.)

"I don't hear you!"

"WALMART!"

"Who is number one?"

"THE CUSTOMER!" (I felt a pang for my mother.)

"Where is the best store?"

"SAINT-LÉONARD!"

The employees screamed, guffawed. Others, like me, wanted to disappear under the floor, uncomfortable at being transformed into cheerleaders for dairy products and toilet plungers. I wondered if I were in a bad corporate video or at a boy scout's jamboree. In the Cubs they would at least have given us marshmallows.

Next, a gazillionth go-round to get to know each other. The new candidates formed a nice, variegated group. Two species of adolescent, those with baby faces and those with acne; vigorous young adults; an undercover journalist (not very vigorous that day); ageless people; and a few sexagenarians who have been around the block. Carmen said that she was 69 years old, including "forty years of direct sales experience." Her neighbour Denise was 62, was a great-grandmother twice over, and offered personal development workshops, which I thought I might need to recover from the pep talk. Jasmin asked her what country she dreamed of visiting. "Going on a trip? Never, I am way too afraid of planes!" shot back Denise.

There was also Nancy, a 38-year-old mother of two, for whom this was a first job. She dreamed of basking on the sands of Bora Bora with her lover. The teens, almost all Haitian or North African, aspired to the same happiness of wealth and trips to Dubai. They wore their golden jewelry, sparkling watches and other bling like ostentatious symbols of a religion which puts its faith in money. These youth also liked joking around and Jasmin called them to order with a sharp and quelling, "Did I say something funny?"

The young executive then went over the safety rules.

"Your health and safety are our priority," he hammered home several times. But clearly not at any price. Or rather, yes, as Jasmin emphasized that even a simple scratch must be reported, at the risk of being penalized. The reason: poorly treated injuries get worse and lead to sick days, and thus decreased productivity. In the same spirit, Jasmin advised against going to the *Commission de la Santé et de la Sécurité du Travail* (Labour Health and Safety Commission or CSST) about injuries. He explained that opening a file there and having a doctor or other specialist intervene would cost the company thousands of dollars.

"Less money in the collective bonus fund," he warned.

"You would do better to come see me. We will find light work for you as you recover from your injury." All the new associates found this idea simple and brilliant.

The company always strongly denied such conduct when I challenged its representatives about it. Walmart Canada's senior director of corporate affairs, Alex Roberton, declared that there was no management directive aimed at discouraging associates from going to the CSST in case of injury.

"The company's priority is always to ensure the health and safety of our employees. Anything that goes against [that] does not reflect store policy,"[1] maintained Roberton.

On the contrary, a former Walmart manager whom I met while writing this book assured me that associates were discouraged from going to the CSST. "Maybe there were instructions to declare the injury," she said, "but it was made clear to the employee that Walmart systematically challenges all CSST decisions, and that if Walmart had to pay anything out, everyone's bonus would be cut."

Ah! The bonus. It is crazy what hold a fistful of money can have over those who have nothing or very little.

"You see that something has spilled on the floor" — Jasmin gave us a scenario — "and you fail to note it in the logbook meant for that purpose. A customer or an associate goes by and hurts themselves by falling on their backside. Walmart risks losing money through a lawsuit or a complaint to the CSST."

In August 2012, a $75,000 lawsuit was launched against a store in Texas after a customer claimed to have been hurt in this way. Such negligence must be avoided; not so much to save the customer's ass as to save Walmart's — and the associate's, because, Jasmin concluded in warning, it would come out of the bonus.

The bonus was not the only thing. Walmart also gave rewards when all employees in the same store succeeded in avoiding an accident for set amount of time. Thirty days: free donuts; sixty days: pizza; ninety days: hot-dog BBQ in the warehouse; 120 days: sugar shack lunch, also in the warehouse. What happens if 150 days go by without an employee being injured?

"No idea because that ceiling has never been reached," answered Jasmin.

I smiled as I wondered if the employees would get to attend a Habs game … in a corner of the warehouse.

At this, Caroline got up and crossed the warehouse to turn out some neon lights before screening a little film on safety. It featured an American "associate" played by an actor who, I'd bet my life, will never be standing on the Dolby theatre stage before his peers, thanking God, the Academy, his charming fourth wife of a quarter of a century, his youngest and his fabulous film crew. The video, entirely devoid of spirit and style, was dubbed and reminiscent of infomercials broadcast late at night to punish insomniacs. The interminable and infantilizing lesson was meant to demonstrate the posture to adopt to avoid injury when lifting heavy objects and how to stand at the cash register without getting back pain.

Jasmin then continued with a presentation of emergency procedures, classified by different codes. The code "Adam" was used when a child is lost. It was named after a real American boy who was kidnapped in a Sears store in Hollywood in 1981. Six-year-old Adam Walsh's mother left the youngster for a few moments near an Atari video game stand. When she came back, the child had disappeared. His body was found a little while later, decapitated. Serial murderer Ottis Toole confessed to the crime but was never convicted due to lack of evidence. Condemned to death for other horrors, he got sick and died in prison. Adam Walsh's father, converted into a lawyer for victims of violent crime, became the celebrity host of the popular show *America's Most Wanted*.

At the Saint-Léonard store, the code Adam was used regularly. Fortunately, it was never kidnapping, but simply children who had escaped their parents' watch and gotten lost in the huge store. As soon as the alert was given, all associates had to leave their work and hunt the aisles. If the child was still missing after ten minutes, all doors were blocked and the police called. Always careful to illustrate his point, Jasmin recounted how a real kidnapping attempt had been thwarted a few years ago in another Montreal store. A man had caught a young girl and put boy's clothes on her before trying to take her out an emergency door. The vigilant employee who barred his way may have saved the child's life.

Code "black" was issued in extreme weather conditions, such as a hurricane. Code "blue" was for bomb alerts, obviously rather rare. There had been several false alarms — all hoaxes — in Quebec over the years, particularly in 2005 when employees at the Jonquière store tried to unionize and Walmart's popularity was at its lowest ebb. Calls to boycott had sounded throughout the province. Even Bernard Landry, former premier of Quebec, publicly stated that he would never set foot in Walmart again, though without encouraging the public to follow suit.

Code "yellow" — signifying an act of violence — was frequently called in the store, which Caroline described as a high-maintenance location. Associates with some experience agreed. Clashes between customers were commonplace. The police regularly came to the store due to theft and fights.

A few weeks later, I witnessed such a scene myself. An older man accidentally stepped on the foot of a customer in his early 30s who angrily retaliated by hitting the old man in the face before running away. In addition to customers, associates were verbally abused, at times even physically. The directive was clear and often repeated: in a situation of aggression, do not respond. Move away and let the security agents deal with the crisis.

The bosses prepared us for real trials from customers. Sometimes excrement was found in the changing rooms or the toy department. And children weren't the only ones responsible. There were also numerous thefts despite the efforts of security agents; there had been more than two hundred interventions the previous year.

Customers were not the only ones in their sights, Caroline added, delivering a severe warning against theft.

"Whether you steal $2 or $100,000, our policy is to bring you to justice. You will get a criminal record and you won't be able to work anywhere. Your life will be ruined," Jasmin threatened.

Caroline expanded: the shop is crawling with cameras, some visible and others, "no bigger than a pin head, able to see customers entering Tim Hortons on the other side of the boulevard and the writing on this bottle of water," shaking it under our rather terrified eyes. Big Brother is watching.

Stealing, moreover, seriously contravenes the company's three fundamental, endlessly repeated, principles: RESPECT FOR THE INDIVIDUAL — SERVICE TO THE CUSTOMER — STRIVE FOR EXCELLENCE.

Associates from twenty-seven countries around the world are sworn to these three maxims, which are like a mantra. Sam Walton first pronounced them in 1962, at the inauguration of the first Walmart

Discount City in Rogers, Arkansas, and there has been no straying from them ever since, it seems. They embody Walmart's corporate culture; but, the more I repeat them, the less I understand their meaning. It's like saying "banana" one hundred times in a row.

But because there are cameras everywhere, I nodded sagely when reminded of the importance of respect for the individual. Working at Walmart is not just a way of paying rent. It is a culture, a way of life, an identity; this is the meaning of the message, I guess. We are entitled to a bunch of privileges as well, on becoming an associate. We are promised that we will get a 10 percent discount in all Walmarts in the world. Morevoer, we will have free access to the physical fitness centre in Bentonville, the company's hometown, should the urge to go lift dumbbells in Arkansas ever overcome us. More intellectually inclined associates can take courses at reduced cost in the Walmart-funded building at Little Rock University.

In reality, for the majority of us, Walmart is limited to the aisles of the Saint-Léonard store. That is not nothing, however. A simple store like the one on Langelier is to the neighbourhood what factories in working-class towns used to be. Its three hundred employees carry out nearly twelve thousand transactions per day and revenues can mount to $400,000 in the holiday season. This formidable cash cow owes its success to customer loyalty and its art of selling them everything: the necessary, the superfluous and the useless. It's a high art form. At Walmart, for example, books are deliberately mixed up on the shelves in order to increase sales. Customers, forced to search to find a specific title, often end up buying two or three others they stumble upon.

Money, money and more money; Walmart's heart seems to beat only to pump out more. We too, bold associates, can aspire to our piece of the pie, continued Caroline, explaining how the shareholding system works. Walmart generously offers to withhold money from our pay each week to buy company shares. The company pays $0.15 per dollar spent on shares by the employee. Each share is currently (as of October 2012) worth about $70 and the company has the wind in its sails, Caroline told us, adding that she put $150 aside each month.

"Each time I go on a trip, I cash in my shares and pay with that!"

The teenagers around the table groaned unhappily when they

learned that they had to be 18 years old to buy shares. They didn't realize that, in any case, virtually no employee would be able to afford them.

The training suddenly took an unexpected turn: environmentalism. Walmart strongly encourages its employees to prepare a "sustainability" plan, because the company advertises itself as "green."

Essentially, each associate must help to make Walmart more environmentally friendly by showing how they are improving the future of the planet through their actions. Nothing less. Join a gym, improve your diet, volunteer, recycle — no action is too small for sustainable development. Employees are required to have a written summary of their sustainability plan on hand because the bosses could ask for it at any time.

Over three months, I did not witness such a request. Nor did I undertake anything of the kind myself. I think I even worsened my ecological footprint. I drove my car to work each day, and I sat down to a plate of junk food more often than ever at one of the restaurants in the shopping mall. Without any scruples. Because when you sweat it out in the bargain kingdom, you find your comfort where you can. And it is true that you use a lot more calories pulling a pallet of milk at Walmart than you do pushing a pen or carting around a microphone at *La Presse*.

That said, the "green" plan is apparently not a complete fabrication. The company's website gives several examples, notably in China in 2012, where 180 children were invited to spend the day at the Shenzhen headquarters and take part in "activities about environmental protection and the meaning of family."[2] A small step in the right direction for China, the world's biggest polluter. Suppliers are also required to make efforts to show green credentials. In Quebec, the paper company Cascades was recognized by Walmart Canada in 2014 for its environmentally responsible practices.

Walmart, we were then told, offers free consultations with a call centre based in Texas called Resources for Living. It is available at any time to discuss personal, professional or dependency problems that associates may face. There is even a guide to help us get a spot in a daycare in our neighbourhood.

Walmart takes good care of you, but woe betide if you transgress one of its many rules. You will face disciplinary measures. The magnanimous employer, however, gives you several chances to make honourable amends before showing you the door. Four, in fact. First, a verbal warning; then a written warning and meeting with a boss; followed by a third written warning and a meeting with two bosses. On a fourth infraction, you are sent home, with pay, to write a statement explaining why the employer should keep you on. This is called a "plan of action" and "the associate had best be convincing!" warned a manager.

After a year, the company clears the slate, setting the counter back to zero. Otherwise all employees would be dismissed, given that they face disciplinary measures for all kinds of offences, from big to the most insignificant: failing to leave your cellphone at the cash; being late; chewing gum; wearing clothes that are dirty or don't conform to the dress code; stealing time by playing around with working hours; stealing full stop. People who protest are also disciplined. It was written in black and white in a little manual distributed to us when we were hired: "It is prohibited to run unnecessarily and to be violent, rude, childlike or contentious when you are at work." Dismissals are rare, said Caroline, trying to be reassuring.

There is no collective agreement establishing a salary scale. Each year, associates undergo a written evaluation to determine their salary increase. The associate is given a mark out of five. Between 0 and 1 means they will have to move mountains to keep their job. From 1 to 2, the associate must improve quickly. From 2 to 3 is so-so. From 3 to 4 is very good and 4 to 4.9 is excellent and worthy of promotion. The score of 5 does not exist because it is perfection and everyone can improve, argued Caroline.

"Even I don't deserve it!" she exclaimed, without irony.

Salary increases are determined by this score and range from $0.10 to $0.50 per hour each year.

The orientation was over. Eight hours had passed. I felt knocked out. I returned to my friends and family at the cottage. It was a drive of a little over two hours, during which time I tried to work out the culture of this strange company. An improbable blend of the iron discipline of the army and the marvelous world of Disney, where Snow White's seven associates whistle as they work.

★ 4 ★

PILGRIMAGE TO WALMARTVILLE

BENTONVILLE (ARKANSAS), SUMMER 1955

Ron Loveless is not yet ten years old and still wears short pants. He lacks a few teeth, but most of all, he lacks strength of character. His older cousin, visiting the house, cheerfully takes advantage of this.

"What if we go steal something at the store," he proposes one day out of sheer boredom.

The Walton's 5&10 is nearby on North Main street in the centre of Bentonville, at that time a mere village in the wilds of northern Arkansas. Ron thinks his cousin's idea fabulous.

The King's latest tune, "That's All Right (Mamma)," was popular on all the juke boxes and playing constantly on the radio. Johnny Cash, a promising young singer, is making himself known with his hit "Cry, Cry, Cry." The country, emerging victorious from the Second World War, is developing at a crazy pace, on all levels, in all directions, so that no one knows where it is going but only that it is going there very quickly, with a smile on its lips and wind in its hair. The wind of prosperity is blowing — even in the remote, rural and poor areas of Arkansas, in the heart of the Bible Belt.

But no one guesses — not even Sam Walton — that in this hilly region, criss-crossed by roads running beside wide fields in which cows graze nonchalantly, the village of Bentonville is about to witness the birth of the most powerful commercial empire in the world. No one, especially not Ron Loveless and his cousin, who are for the moment only interested in stealing a knife from the general store. The operation is a success … for the moment. That very afternoon, Ron's mother discovers the stolen knife in the pocket of her young son's pants. Having spent many years in the service of the Waltons as a cleaning woman, she would never dream of leaving this crime unpunished. She drags young Ron by the ear all the way to the store, to return the knife to its owner. Two weeks later, Sam Walton pays a visit to the young thief's mother in person, bearing a small, white puppy.

"Here, give it to the boy, maybe it will stop him from making mistakes," the shopkeeper said.

The sequel belongs to Walmart's official history.

After the larceny, Sam Walton became fond of the boy, finding him his first job stocking goods in his store. A few years later, in 1962, Sam Walton opened the very first Walmart Discount City, in a neighbouring farming village, a hamlet of barely five hundred people called Rogers. "Wal-Mart, Discount City, Guaranteed Quality and Discount Prices" proclaimed a sign out front. This was the beginning of a tremendous ascent for Walmart, which would carry Ron Loveless to the top position of Sam's Club, a major subsidiary of the multinational. For the young man, the crime paid off in the end. Ron Loveless recounts his incredible journey in *Walmart Inside Out: From Stockboy to Stockholder*.[1] It's the story of a kid who had nothing, whose very name (Loveless) speaks of exclusion. But then he is touched by the grace of financial success. He is saved. Elected. He was only a stockboy, a stevedore, a needy person stagnating on the lowest rung of human society. Walmart granted him the dignity of shareholder, of stockholder; hoisted him to the demiurgic status of boss. Before, he had to work to receive money in the form of a salary, now money works for him: he receives dividends. To all associates, his story testifies to the hope implicit in Walmart's economic power.

I met Loveless more than sixty years after the theft of the knife that catapulted him onto the road to success. He welcomed my videographer colleague Ninon and me into his opulent home on the edge of a pretty wooded area. He received us warmly. We first spoke about Sam Walton, practically a father to Ron Loveless, who had never known his own.

"For me, one word describes Sam Walton: studious. He never stopped listening. When you spoke to him, you had the impression that he understood nothing about business, that he had everything to learn," recounted Loveless, who left the company at only 42, to move on to other challenges. He became a consultant for various companies.

Our host no longer bore any resemblance to the young scamp he once was — a little lost and easily influenced. Meticulous hair and an impeccable suit as vividly blue as the eyes shining through his small round glasses. When we raised the numerous criticisms leveled at his former boss, Loveless took his part and offered another way of seeing things, "He didn't want to destroy the competition, he just wanted to be the best."

His mentor died in 1992. A few months previously, he had been awarded the Presidential Medal of Freedom, the highest civilian award in the United States. He received this honour at the hands of President George Bush (Sr.). The president, visibly emotional on the podium, hailed the contribution of this man, a true incarnation of the American dream.

"The story of Sam Walton is an illustration of the American dream. His success is our success, America's success. And when Sam's grandchildren read about what makes America great, they'll read about people who have grand ideas and great dreams, resourceful people who make imagination come alive with accomplishment," declared the head of state, a tremor in his voice.

Sam Walton, already weakened by long illness (leukemia), wearing a baseball cap with the company logo, used this final forum to publicly announce that Walmart would continue its global conquest.

"If we work together, we'll lower the cost of living for everyone … we'll give the world an opportunity to see what it's like to save and have a better life."[2]

Even on the verge of death, the man was one of the most powerful people in the world. To the point that the President of the United States and his wife traveled to his town to pay him the nation's homage.

Several years previously, Sam Walton had been named the richest man in America. This title seemed to catch everyone somewhat by surprise, including the principal.

"Success has always had its price, I guess, and I learned that lesson the hard way in October of 1985 when *Forbes* magazine named me the so-called 'richest man in America.' Well it wasn't too hard to imagine all those newspaper and TV folks up there in New York saying, 'Who?' and 'He lives where?'"[3]

Despite the homey image of the billionaire who continued to get his hair cut at the local barber shop, his achievement was such that the republic bowed down low before him. His heirs, who own about 40 percent of the company's shares, are twice as rich as Bill Gates' family.[4]

The cows still graze in the hilly pastures around Bentonville as though nothing has changed since 1955. This pastoral mirage deceives no one, however: it is Walmart that makes the milk and honey flow in the region now, and in the entire country.

"More than 20,000 of our fellow citizens wake up every morning to go to work at Walmart," boasted the mayor of Bentonville, Bob McCaslin, comfortably installed in an armchair in an office that could have come out of a *Mad Men* set.

This sexagenarian mayor didn't hold back on his praise for the global giant, whose head office was just a few blocks away. "It's an honour to be the mayor of a city that is home to the biggest retailer in the world," cried McCaslin, who was elected in 2007.

Walmart has the reputation of wiping out small shopping streets and reducing downtown cores to no man's lands, but it has not altered the charms of its alma mater. The thirty-six thousand residents of Bentonville have kept the old buildings and the churches of diverse denomination on each street corner and preserved the architecture that makes small towns picturesque. There is also the famous southern hospitality. Benton County is considered the most lenient of the dry (alcohol-free) counties, even though people must still go to the neighbouring state of Missouri to buy alcohol.

However, no description of the scene would be complete without mention of the omnipresence of Walmart: the head office, the boulevard, the museums, the university building … the company's mark is everywhere. The many red brick buildings that house the company's offices are scattered throughout the city. The grounds of the main building border a cemetary and a rather dilapidated residential neighbourhood, whose streets have letters instead of names.

In front of the head office, at the corner of 8th Street and Walton Boulevard, a huge luminous sign announces, "Saving you money is our number one mission." Inside the building, in a large and spacious lobby like a waiting room in a private clinic, period photos and company artefacts hang on the walls under glass: a complete retrospective of the history of Walmart, like the Way of the Cross revisited and shorn of the manifest suffering of martyrdom, reminding America that one can obtain success in ten stations.

Security agents cruise the area in patrol cars. Business people hang around in the waiting room. Most are representatives of one of the 1300 companies that maintain a foothold in the area in order to be close to their most important client. Suppliers come from all over the world to court Her Majesty Walmart. Visitors had better be well prepared. Negotiations are difficult and direct. Bentonville refuses intermediaries.

"When they get there, sellers are installed without ceremony in small rooms, more like monastic cells than comfortable meeting rooms. One table, four chairs. No formalities: Walmart gets straight to the point."[5]

In their reflection *Walmart: L'entreprise-monde* (*Walmart: Company-World*), Nelson Lichtenstein and Susan Strasser go further. They explain that, for the first time in the history of modern capitalism, an entrepreneurial model has made the retailer the king and the manufacturer his vassal. "The company has thus transformed a large number of its suppliers into pleading and trembling 'partners', forced to scramble to reduce costs and wring the last drop of productive sweat out of millions of workers and subcontractors."[6]

In addition to the billions of dollars they transact with Walmart, these modern vassals benefit the local economy of Bentonville, where they arrive in droves.

"They buy houses, raise their families, register their children in our schools," rejoiced the elderly mayor McCaslin.

The suppliers and their families have also left local commercial life intact: kitsch car-washes, drive-ins frozen in time, and dilapidated houses stubbornly maintaining a storefront. The museum, constructed on the very spot where Sam Walton opened his first store after the War, houses a 1950s-décor snack bar, a tribute to the era of the company's birth and its creator's unconditional love for ice cream. Especially butterscotch ice cream, says museum director Alan Dranow, who knows the founder's biography by heart.

"He was larger than life. Everyone loved him," summed up this unwavering disciple.

The museum has assembled the company's relics: the famous medal awarded to Sam Walton by George Bush, Sr.; his wife's wedding dress; Sam's office, left untouched; and the old 1979 Ford pickup truck that Sam kept until his death.

"Why do I drive a pickup truck? What am I supposed to haul my dogs around in, a Rolls Royce?"[7] he liked to repeat.

The humility of the person who rambled around in his old pickup was sincere, Ron Loveless confirmed, and when you walk down the sidewalkless streets of Bentonville, you find that Walmart doesn't look the part of a money-pumping mega-corporation. Quite the contrary. The closer you get to the head office, the more you feel you are dealing with a warm, local company reflecting family and community values. In fact, the entire city seems to have adopted the humility and frugality of Sam Walton, proving the myth true: the excess of the capitalist company doesn't prevent anyone from leading a simple and authentic human life.

"I'm not sure I ever really figured out this celebrity business. Why in the world, for example, would I get an invitation to Elizabeth Taylor's wedding out in Hollywood? I still can't believe it was news that I get my hair cut at the barbershop. Where else would I get it cut?"[8]

Because they were personally in contact with the entrepreneur and his family, the citizens of Bentonville feel they played a part in this history. This is true of Peggy Hamilton, still working for Walmart at nearly 70 years old. She met "Mr. Sam" in 1971, at the opening of store no. 34 in Nevada, where she worked in the women's clothing department.

"He always asked me what was selling. He offered me a managerial position at the head office," explained this petite woman, who witnessed the incredible boom transform her region over the decades.

"People from around here are proud to share this beautiful history with people," she summed up.

But what currently makes residents of the area swell with pride is the Crystal Bridges museum, opened in 2012 and funded almost entirely by Walmart. Sam Walton's daughter, the eccentric Alice, is the patron of this impressive project into which the company poured $20 million. She is known locally in Bentonville as the "white wolf." Everyone has glimpsed her at least once driving one of her innumerable sports cars at breakneck speeds in the area. This driving fanatic has been involved in many accidents, including a fatal one in 1989. Driving her Porsche, Alice Walton struck and killed Oleta Hardin. The victim, a mother of two children, had ventured out into the lane of the highway on which she lived. Alice Walton was also caught intoxicated several times. The last time was in 2011 in Texas, on her 62nd birthday. Texan crown attorneys dropped the charges two years later. Alice Walton's scrapes have not prevented her young museum from achieving a phenomenal success. The architect of this state-of-the-art art gallery, built at the bottom of a forested ravine, is none other than Moshe Safdie, the architect of Habitat '67. Visitors can contemplate the works of Andy Warhol, Georgia O'Keefe and John Singer Sargent. Entry to the museum is free and must remain so according to the patron's wish. Despite Walmart's considerable contribution, there is almost no trace of the company on site. This was a *sine qua non* condition in Alice Walton's eyes, according to the museum's public relations person, Diane Carroll. Walmart's action here was disinterested, "Purely from love of art and a gift to the community!"

Gary Welborn admits that he gets his share of the fruits of this gift. Driving his taxi, he brings clients to the museums, restaurants and hotels cropping up in the city.

"I have clients from Africa, India, Brazil, Canada and the Middle East. Walmart is a success story which people from here saw unfold before their eyes," proudly proclaims the 53-year-old, who also worked for Walmart for several years. He met "Mr. Sam" several times at store no. 54 in Springdale, where he was a manager. Also a pastor, he went to preach in a Detroit church for seventeen years before returning to the area in 1999.

Voices critical of the company are rare in Bentonville. A few barbs about working conditions here and there, but they are half-hearted. Even Gary Welborn, who unsuccessfully tried to start a competing company in Bentonville before becoming a taxi driver, does not accuse Walmart of wiping out all the competition.

"If you want to fight, you will lose. To survive, you have to collaborate and offer complementary services," the pastor believes.

In his view, it is normal for the company, number one in the world, to come under fire, but one shouldn't lose sight of what it has done well, nor of what would happen if it were no longer there: "If Walmart closed it would dry up the region, like I saw in Detroit when the automobile giants closed down."

Mayor McCaslin likes to compare Walmart's success to a hockey team's.

"It takes discipline and the best players. Walmart has both," the mayor believes, critizing the media for peddling a negative image of the retailer.

"People come here to tell us how to treat and pay our employees. But Walmart has never forced anyone to work there. I know because my son-in-law works at Walmart and he has never told me that he is chained to his desk."

Walmart may be perceived as a threat. Ron Loveless recognizes this. Yes, small businesses have difficulty surviving where the giant sets up shop. But the real mission of Walmart, as imagined by Sam Walton, lies in this close relationship between the retailer and the community, his former protégé explained.

"The further removed from Walmart's basic territory, the tougher it is to understand Walmart, the deeper the misconception," conceded Loveless. He added that he is not completely opposed to unions but is suspicious that they fight more for their own interests. He believes that unions somewhat skew the American dream.

"I started at the bottom of the ladder, I hardly had enough money to buy milk for my baby. I succeeded thanks to my efforts."

The implication: unions would have made me less poor but would have barred the path leading to the highest rungs.

Walmart clothes itself in voluntary simplicity, in a somewhat improvised, almost rustic, conviviality, but do not misunderstand: the company is an impressive, ultra-modern war machine, in which nothing is left to chance. Absolutely nothing. The cleverly maintained gap between the rural Bentonville atmosphere and the firm's high-tech dimension, established by Sam Walton, forms the backdrop to an essay by Nelson Lichenstein and Susan Strasser on the multinational. "It's the Walmart paradox: how did one of the most backwater areas of America become the headquarters of the global company we know today?"[9]

Walmart's IT budget is bigger than NASA's.[10] The Bentonville head office, as remote as it is, controls the logistics of all Walmart stores. Basically, all decisions are validated, everything is controlled from there; even the temperature of the fridges in a Montreal store.

"Walmart's representatives can maintain the image of a virtuous company, where Christian family values, community spirit and equality dominate, as so many 'ideological tropes'. This remains despite the striking contrast between this 'managerial ethos' inherited from the most conservative fringes of the Republican Party and the sophistication of the technological resources at its disposal, which in reality translate into an invisible management."[11]

Walmart is still several leagues ahead of its competitors in the great race for the technological revolution. In the mid-1960s, when the company only had around twenty stores, its executives went head hunting to an IBM school, seeking out the most brilliant students capable of using emerging technologies to help Walmart outstrip the competition.

"Eight years later, it was equipped with the biggest private communications network in the country. A very advanced data exchange system with its suppliers — Electronic Data Interchange — has become Walmart's hallmark, the mechanism by which it cuts costs, saves time by eliminating paperwork (everything being done electronically), and eliminates errors in ordering."[12]

In the 1980s, Walmart became the first company to purchase a network of private satellites to ensure permanent contact between all stores and the head office. The cost of this satellite system was $24 billion.

The multinational has "an approach based on costs and customer satisfaction. Walmart simply has the technology to apply this model," explained JoAnne Labrecque, HEC Montreal professor specializing in retail business. Shipping a product from China to America is now so commonplace that we think of it as easy.

"It seems simple," said Labrecque, "but it requires operational genius." Walmart's good fortune owes a lot to the company's domination on the logistical front. Walmart, she declared, "is efficiency. It is not a company, it's a machine."

A machine that can calculate and measure anything, even the average number of products scanned by each cashier (between four hundred and five hundred per hour). Walmart's telecommunications system allows constant and direct management of the flow of merchandise everywhere in the world and evaluation of store productivity with surgical precision.

"Thanks to their know-how, the logistic gurus at head office in Bentonville know at all times where merchandise is and where stocks are. In real time, they can arbitrate at the global level, putting workers in South Carolina in competition with workers in Southern China and factories in Baltimore, Maryland in competition with those in Bangalore, India to better place orders."[13]

Walmart cannot put the brakes on; its existence depends on escalating this omnidirectional control. The company is now a pioneer in the field of radio-frequency chips (or radio tags), JoAnne Labrecque informed me. Walmart has never made a secret of its intention to require all its suppliers to outfit their products with these radio identification devices, which allow customers to be tracked as they shop. Without the knowledge of customers, a controversial experiment was conducted in 2003 in conjuction with Proctor & Gamble, who equipped lipstick with radio-frequency chips. The products were sold in a store in Tulsa, Oklahoma. When clients put this lipstick in their cart, a marketing department manager of the cosmetics company was able spy on them via surveillance cameras throughout the store, thus tracking their consumer behaviour in detail.

Walmart's genius consists of staying on the cutting edge of cybernetic systems of control while projecting an image of a completely down-to-earth company in its business practices. On one side, the rule of computers and satellites; on the other, unbridled customer passions, common sense, the virtues of work and individual effort. Ron Loveless, when he was vice president of the company, helped nurture this image with his famous chicken patrol story, a joke he made at a congress in Arkansas when asked how Walmart estimated market demand for products on sale. Instead of talking about its computer system, he said, "You see, when times are good, you find plenty of dead chickens by the side of the road, ones that have fallen off the truck. But when times are getting lean, people stop and pick up the dead chickens and take 'em home for dinner. So in addition to traditional methods, we try to correlate our advance stock orders with the number of dead chickens by the side of the road."[14]

The chicken patrol was a joke but it says a great deal about Walmart's image. It presents a proletarian face to its customers, while operating NASA-calibre tools to pull strings in the shadows, like the Wizard of Oz. The customers who continue to pile into its parking lots, lured by the low prices, see nothing. Just like the cows grazing in the pastures around Bentonville.

ALI BABA AND THE $600 OF MOTOR OIL

SAINT-LÉONARD WALMART, OCTOBER 9, 2012

Today I served fifty customers before my lunch break. The usual routine. Demand is permanent. It is urgent, exacting, noisy, often suffocating. I feel like Justin Bieber in a surprise visit to a day camp, minus the cries of joy and the autographs. As soon as I begin to serve one customer, another accosts me; as I go to the item the first demanded, the second follows and two more join en route. We end up moving around in clusters.

My morning was nighmare-esque because I was not yet familiar with how products were distributed among the various sections.

"Excuse me sir, where are the coffee filters?"

"Row 4, under the large sign saying coffee …"

"Do you have iced of sugar?"

"Huh?"

"Iced of sugar! ICED OF SUGAR!!"

"Ah! Icing sugar! Row 5, with the cake mixes."

Questions in French, in English, in Spanish, in Italian. Excuse me, do you work here? (Umh. You see my bright blue vest with "Walmart" written on it?) Do you have tires? The liquor on sale has run out, do you have more in the back? Can you give me a discount on this since it wasn't on the right shelf? Where are the coffee machines? J-cloths? Jute to protect trees? Do you have $600 worth of W5/30 motor oil? Vanilla extract? Your nerves have to be steady to withstand the bombardment.

In the customer's imagination, the warehouse is a kind of Ali Baba's cave abounding with coveted treasure. If we explain that a product is absent from the shelves because there is no more in stock, they systematically exhort us to "go look in the back," because the idea that a product could run out appears scandalous to them. One specimen, incensed at not finding the discounted screwdriver announced in the flyer, theatrically tore up the flyer in front my eyes, before leaving the store in a fury.

My colleagues faced the mob with Olympian calm.

"Didn't I tell you? Just try to imagine holidays and weekends," whispered one of them in my ear.

My supervisor asked me to put up posters listing sales prices at the end of each aisle in the immense store. The task was long, repetitive and depressing. I had to lug a stepladder down the aisles, zigzagging the customers who, to my chagrin, continued to accost me. I couldn't ignore them. I had to obey the "three metre" rule: the associate must smile at all times and when a customer is within three metres, the associate must greet the customer, ask if they need help and, if necessary, escort them to the product. After being abused by several customers, I found this rule painful to respect. The customer has little consideration for the associate, to say the least.

I passed an older couple boldly opening a box containing a coffee machine to see what kind of filter it used.

"Um, you aren't supposed to open the boxes."

"Come on, you make tons of money here," retorted the woman in a hard tone.

No denying she's right. But is that any reason to brush me off like that? She or her husband finally decided the coffee filter was compatible with the machine and went to the cash. Two more satisfied customers. I took my break with a feeling of duty accomplished.

Late by four minutes after my break, I felt delinquent. Today I received my card and slid it through the electronic time stamp for the first time. I felt light years away from *La Presse*, where time is elastic and it is normal to sit down at any time to sip a latté with colleagues and discuss weekend plans, an interesting read, juicy gossip or a future story that may never see the light of day. We only feel time pressure when the deadline for the newspaper approaches.

I was asked to put the dairy products in the newly installed fridges so that I became familiar with my future environment. This was to be done before the big inauguration of the new food section. I was on familiar terrain. It was child's play to shelve the three pallets of food brought to me and I confess to a nostaligic pleasure. The smell of the warehouse, the pallet truck, the noise of the knife blade through the cardboard boxes: it all brought me back to my old life in a Saint-Eustache supermarket. I remember the cashier, Anna, her beauty such that she resisted the affront (or dictatorship?) of the baggy beige pants imposed on us, making her a non-negligible work incentive for the hormone-doped teen I was. And our customers of the time? Warm, mostly neighbours, always polite.

Walmart customers are not the associates' neighbours but, just like them, people of modest means. It occurred to me that Walmart, in its great generosity, paid its employees to give its customers the illusion that they are ordering around beings even lower than they are on the social ladder. Our obligation to kowtow to them gives them a taste of the joys of power.

But still, do they have to treat us like doormats?

★

In the meeting the following morning, it was announced that sales figures for the previous day were only $129,000 — much less than the same day one year ago. And the share price of Walmart fell by a dollar. Very bad news, but not insurmountable. Go, roll up your sleeves, gang! We will do better today! W! A! L! … The bosses are free to trot out their two-cent psychology to try to stimulate us, but there is no way I am going to feel guilty for yesterday's "meager" profits.

Yesterday I made $88. Gross.

The morning meetings are also an opportunity to celebrate birthdays and hiring anniversaries. We learned that it had been eleven years since Solange began working at the store. An important milestone like that is pinned to the employee's badge, like a military decoration. Proud to have served you for ten years.

For many of my colleagues, Walmart was not only life history but family history as well. In Solange's case, her daughter Karine was hired at the same time I was. Nancy had a brother working nights in the warehouse. They crossed paths each morning. Christian's mother was also on the night shift. These two were cute. Despite his tough appearance, Christian religiously hugged his mother every morning when their shifts overlapped.

After Solange's badge was decorated, Barry, the imposing guy in charge of renovations, used the morning meeting to summarize progress on construction. In English only, which didn't appear to annoy any of the associates present, almost all francophone.

Back in the store, the customers were especially aggressive. The new flyer had come out, but many of the items were not yet on the shelves. Many customers had waited in their cars in the parking lot for the store to open — determined to give us no respite. One of them was scandalized that he could not find a set of eighteen dessert plates. As often as we repeated that there were none in stock, he returned to the charge, distraught: "But what I am going to do? Eh? What will I do?" (You could throw yourself off the Champlain bridge or wait there until it collapses, because your life seems to have lost all meaning.)

"You could consult our online catalogue to see if one of the other stores has it in stock."

Disgruntled, he turned on his heel without a word of thanks. I had just struggled to calm his anxiety attack for a good fifteen minutes. Politely letting him annoy the hell out of me, repeating over and over in my head one of the fundamental laws of the associate: "The customer is my boss, the customer is my boss, the customer is my boss …"

Thankfully, there were also nice and colourful customers, like an old lady of Italian origin who called to me in her mother tongue and came alive in caricature fashion when she saw I did not understand what she was saying. For my part, I added "a"s and "o"s to the end of my words and she redoubled her miming efforts; so effectively that at last I understood that she was looking for yeast. Her face lit up when I handed her a package.

"Grazie, grazie! Per la pizza!"

The Italian mama who wanted to make pizza at 9:00 a.m. Classic.

Customers make me see all colours, but today it was not customers who made me fear the worst. A little before my lunch break, the intercom sounded my name throughout the store, "Hugo from the dairy section to the staff office."

"Damn, busted!" I thought. Already?

I went to the staff office like someone condemned to death, convinced that my bosses had discovered the truth. It was just a matter of time; every day I told myself that I was just a Google search away from being found out.

Still, I derived a malicious pleasure from ignoring the customer trotting along behind me, crying, "Sir! Sir!" If you are about to be fired for being an undercover journalist, there's no need to be overly zealous.

I entered the office long-faced. Caroline and her human resources colleague sported broad smiles, which added to my anxiety.

"Have you heard about the modules?"

HOLD ON, HUGO!

"Modules" is the name given to a series of short lessons administered to Walmart associates via a computer programme. It is difficult to describe these mandatory training exercices. An interminable, infantilizing ordeal that, to add insult to injury, took place on a Soviet-era computer at the back of a windowless office, cluttered and dusty. It was going to be a long day.

Modules are divided into themes: recycling, blood infections, cardboard compacter, protective tools, sexual harassment and so forth. The text is riddled with errors and the French appears to have been translated by antediluvian software. Each module is presented by an improbable animated character straight out of an Atari or a pixelated nightmare. This talking thing introduces itself as an "employee" of a Canadian store. Any dunce could easily come up with a better graphic animation.

Nor are the exercises any more advanced. I started, for example, by having to dress our friend Steven by clicking on appropriate clothing.

We are then shown how to make bales of recycled plastic. A "friendly" character, inspired by an Ontario associate extremely concerned about recycling (bordering on obsession), joyfully rebaptizes these bales "plastic sandwich balls."

He repeats the expression a dozen times. In a bad animated interaction, the recycling associate invites a colleague to throw the bales into some kind of a container.

"You see, Keisha, you can have fun and save the planet at the same time!" cries the enviro employee excitedly.

"Wow I feel like an NBA (pronounced in an accent from France) player!" exclaims the sensitized employee.

For the first time since beginning my infiltration, I came within a hair's breadth of quitting my new work and returning to normal journalistic practices. Lots of my colleagues were having fun pulling skeletons out of the huge closet in the worlds of construction and politics at that time. To say that I felt disgruntled watching Keisha throwing plastic sandwich balls into a container would be a gross understatement.

Hold on, Hugo! You are not going to let yourself be taken out by cartoons.

The module on sexual harassment made me downright aggressive. The scenarios, designed to sensitize us to the issue, were as predictable as the coyote's half-baked schemes against Bugs Bunny. Ali pumped up his disproportionate chest and made advances towards a young hiree of alluring pixels. If she refused his advances, he threatened, he would tell everyone that she had gone out with him.

"Is this sexual harassment?" asked the screen.

"Yes," answered our worthy virtual presenter before giving a lengthy explanation.

In the next scene, we see a badly dressed Ali, face defeated, standing in front of his boss, who is grabbing his blue vest with both hands. "When you said that you would tell everyone that she had gone out with you, that was a threat," the boss sternly reproached him, literally showing him the door with an accusing finger.

"A compliment on a colleague's physical appearance is sexual harassment: yes or no?" asks the Soviet computer. The right response: yes, if we compliment a little too enthusiastically. The company does not take the fight against sexual harassment lightly; it even prohibits its employees from bringing magazines, calendars and cartoons to work. Walmart also prohibits managers from going out with associates, to avoid abuse of power or any form of favouritism. Walmart does not prohibit love but love is only permitted if employees hold the same rank in the hierarchy.

The sexual harassment module then portrayed a female manager asking a male associate to go out with her. Suffering a refusal, the boss' pixelated eyebrows frowned.

"The annual evaluation is approaching and you will get a better mark if you go out with me," warned the perfidious manager, in tailored clothes. Should such a situation arise — even if it seems as unlikely as the craziest fantasies of a pizza delivery man — the associate is invited to report the malefactor to the highest levels of the company.

The open-door rule is always in effect at Walmart. We can always go to see a boss in the store, the district or even the Toronto headquarters to discuss a problem of harassment. All of their numbers are posted everywhere on billboards. The principle seems excellent to me, but it didn't make the modules any more bearable.

Caroline heard me sighing as she passed the desk where I was bitterly tasting the absurdity of the world and stopped to slip me a word of encouragement, "The goal of these modules is to make you want to go back to work in the store."

You know what? It works!

★

Sales were at $129,000 yesterday, again lower than the same date last year. However, shares went up by a dollar, leading to a round of applause during the morning meeting. Book sales were apparently going really well. Big thanks to the bestsellers *Fifty Shades of Grey* and a new J.K. Rowling novel, which were selling like hotcakes.

After lunch, one of the managers called me as I entered the back of the store with my bag on my shoulder.

"Hey, Hugo, when you enter and leave with a bag, you have to go by the staff room, not the side door. Nothing personal, but just in case."

In case of what, exactly? In case I was lugging around a laptop in which I was noting all the gleanings of my journalistic spying during breaks? Mwahahaha! Coming back into the store, I busied myself arranging the displays at the end of each aisle. The Maxwell House coffee on promotion had to be replaced by jars of Catelli tomato sauce, also on sale. A marketing strategy, I'm told. I guess more intelligent people than I have carefully reflected on this maneouver, which nevertheless seems a waste of time. A customer burst my bubble. He was annoyed that there was no more oil on sale on a shelf which had been stripped bare. I sympathized with his misfortune and offered him a ray of hope, that we would receive several pallets in the next order.

"Yes, but what am I supposed to do until then? Camp out in front of the store to be sure to get one?" he retorted dryly. (You can build a bungalow in the aisle if that turns you on, I couldn't care less.)

"Ha! Ha! What an excellent joke, sir! If you would like, I can contact the closest store to see if there are any left in stock."

The man glared at me and left grumbling. Worse than a child! "I waaaaaaant my oil!" The customer is always right.

The day dragged on. Marc, the manager, complimented me on my work. I was not too rusty, it was true. The reflexes came back quickly. I had to admit that it felt good to do a little physical work and also that I was treated well, minus the customers and the modules. A strange feeling of well-being overcame me. Was I in the process of becoming attached to my new livelihood? Developing a new kind of Stockholm syndrome? The Bentonville syndrome, characterized by an unexpected surge of affection by the associate for his master, Walmart?

In any case, I am the type to be satisfied with little. When a Cora restaurant offered me my first opportunity as a dishwasher when I was a teenager, I was able to stay on my feet there for two years and if the franchise hadn't gone bankrupt, I might still be there. The owner, a round, unscrupulous woman (no causal link between the two), fled south with the employees' petty cash. This put an end to my career as a dishwasher. The staff found out at 6:00 a.m. one Saturday morning from a small sign posted on the front door: "Closed due to bankruptcy." I had played the responsible teenager the night before, leaving the drinking party at the Martel sisters' earlier than usual in order to be operational at work. Anyway.

A few months before the restaurant closed, however, my younger self, long hair imprisoned in a net, had tried to improve my working conditions: "Yo ma'am, I, like, want to be like a server or busboy, I am sick of being just a dishwasher." (Note: I didn't really say "yo" or "like," but I am attempting teen speak.) The owner answered, "Pull yourself together, my little Hugo (I was still puny). You are not just a dishwasher, you are THE dishwasher!"

Galvinized by this inspiring speech, I returned to dishwashing; scraping egg yolks off plates with renewed vigour. The smile that Marc's compliment put on my face made me think that I hadn't lost my beautiful naiveté. One thing was sure, my new fellows and bosses were pretty nice. My department manager, Stephanie, was like a fish in water in this dysfunctional universe, and much beloved by her troops.

Before leaving, she whispered to me to skip tomorrow's meeting. "Go finish off your modules. Frozen goods come in on Monday."

★

It was still night when I forced open the store's disactivated electric doors. I had first made a stop at the Tim Hortons on the other side of the street, which seemed to be besieged by a line-up twenty-four-hours a day.

No question of going into the store with a Starbucks Venti Latte worth a half-hour of work. In any case, the American coffee giant was still closed at this indecent hour. I reflected that customers who have the resources to pay five bucks for coffee certainly had no need to get up in the middle of the night to go work.

I had to take similar precautions with my car, which I parked far from the entrance to avoid being seen by colleagues who could not afford the "luxury" of their own vehicle. The majority were at the mercy of the terrible night bus schedule to get to work on time. And during the breaks, better to smoke cheap cigarettes — Pall Mall or Indians — to blend in.

My day started once again on an old Soviet computer. The machine told me how to behave towards people with handicaps and others with a variety of health issues. The lesson applied to relations with customers as well as staff, which included several people with intellectual disabilities. Another sign of the openness and integration of the company, the Saint-Léonard store also employed an amputee and a transsexual. Several veiled women numbered among my colleagues. They were regularly subject to racist comments by the customers (we should have sold them training modules).

Associates of colour also came in for their share of derogatory comments. "I asked her where the vertical blinds were and she didn't know. Probably they don't know what they are for in their country!" a customer whispered to me in a tone of *pure laine*[1] complicity, pointing with her chin to a colleague of Haitian origin.

A useful module at last! This one promised to show me how to remain courteous to customers, because a happy customer is a customer who returns. False hope. The virtual simulation proved to be one of the most distressing. The exercise consisted of clicking as quickly as possible on two-dimensional clients who appeared here and there on the screen. Each time I succeeded in matching the speed of this paleolithic software — which my four-year-old son would have been able to do blindfolded with one hand tied behind his back — the virtual customer gave a big smile and $100 flashed on the side of the screen.

Unsurprisingly, money was the basis of all the training modules. Recycling brings in money; being polite does too; and so does respecting health and safety rules. An employee in good shape is a productive employee. A customer spends an average of $100 per week at Walmart. The computer's conclusion after an astute calculation (precise to the point of subtracting two weeks of vacation per year): each customer brings in about $5,000. The customer was thus our number one priority. In the United States, 90 percent of Americans live within twenty-five km (fifteen miles) of a Walmart and each average family of four spends about $4,000 per year there, according to *Business Insider*.[2] Finished off by a module on violence in which a quarrel between an associate and his brother, who came to the store to hassle him, ended in a massive police intervention, I took a break.

They gave us donuts. There hadn't been an accident for thirty days.

DIARY OF AN ASSOCIATE I

CAT AND MOUSE

October 15, 2012

Marc, the manager, was like a cat who just swallowed a mouse. The first pallets of frozen food had just arrived. It was a historic moment for the Saint-Léonard Walmart, nine days away from its big inauguration. Marc shook my hand vigorously, convinced that I shared his joy. He gave commands in the feverish tone of a captain giving the order to cast off in a bid to conquer the world: "Stock is low. We should increase it. But not more than five pallets at a time."

An army of associates had been conscripted to fill the still virgin shelves of the new section. Associates had even been sent from other stores in the area as reinforcements. The success of the operation relied on speed, because we had to avoid letting the products thaw. I moved the loaded pallets, stacked ten feet high. I drove the assault tanks, so to speak; a dangerous exercise because I had to zigzag between goods scattered around the warehouse and then move rapidly to the battle station: the freezers. As soon as I arrived, a battalion of associates threw themselves on the pallet, grabbing frozen juice, butter, Pogos, fries and vegetables — and of course the ice cream.

I seized boxes in threes, placing them in front of the right displays to simplify the stocking clerks' work a little. Christian slowed me down.

"Calm down, man, one box at a time. We're paid by the hour. There's no rush."

He moved calmly, as though he were wandering around a museum, making me look like a workaholic in comparison. His intervention was most effective. After all, he was completely right: why should I put my back out for a minimum-wage job? The company would continue to rake in the millions, whether or not I pushed myself.

All of these emotions made me hungry. I ate lunch at a Thai restaurant beside the famous Chinese buffet Le Mandarin. I took the opportunity of recording my daily observations in my computer, sitting at a table near the back, trembling with fear of being caught in the act each time a new customer burst into the room. I don't have James Bond's cool. Nor his pectorals, alas.

Returning to the store, I stopped at the *tabagie*[1] to buy smokes. The employee noticed the blue vest I had scrunched in one hand and suddenly became very polite. An employee of the mall is a customer who returns.

Walmart isn't the only one with a knack for business.

EIGHT DAYS AND FORTY-SEVEN MINUTES

October 16, 2012

We were given a little surprise. This morning it was the boss of the store, François, who announced yesterday's sales figures to us. It was the first time I saw him in the flesh. His reputation was that of a severe but fair man.

"If you do your job, you won't have any trouble with him," said Christian.

He was about my age, with a well-trimmed beard and curly hair. We looked a little alike; so much so, in fact, that several colleagues asked if we were related.

He took the opportunity to remind us that the grand opening of the supercentre was coming up very soon. "In eight days and forty-seven minutes. Is anyone here not stressed by that?" he asked, taking for granted that we were as anxious about it as he was. Then he went on to announce that if anyone wanted to make a pie or a cake, now would be an ideal time, because the large bags of flour were going on sale tomorrow. Several female colleagues rejoiced and exchanged their favourite recipes.

A manager then opened a big box containing small slippers for children and babies. "Look at them, we just got them. Each pair costs $8 and we will make more than 60 percent profit on it," enthused the manager, moved by such a beautiful profit margin. He tossed the baby shoes to employees who caught them; whether charmed by the product or the profits, I wasn't sure.

After the frozen goods, pallets of dairy products made their entrance. Eggs, milk, cheese and yogurt in industrial quantities. Marc again had difficulty containing his joy.

"You're in your element there, Hugo!" he called, passing me as I placed Tropicana mango juice on the refrigerated shelves. "Yes, boss!"

Time passes very quickly when things go smoothly. There is even a certain satisfaction when work yields good results. The proverbial feeling of duty accomplished. The shelves filled up day after day. The section took shape.

My section.

A colleague from another store came to help me as I put Sunny Delight juice bottles on the shelves. Well past fifty, she works at a Laval store. She lives a stone's throw away from my store but would never work here. "With the customers here, I don't think so!" She worked for Bell for thirty years before being forced into an early retirement, with a modest financial compensation. Three years later, she went back to work. She had no choice.

She burst into laughter when I told her that I had been working there for three weeks.

"Well then, my friend, you've seen nothing yet."

TEACHER'S PET FILLS
THE FROZEN GOODS SHELVES

October 17, 2012

At the meeting, the boss gave an update on the competition. New Walmart stores would be opening in the sector as quickly as possible, he told us, in a bid to outpace Giant Tiger, which was moving our way. This other American colossus retailer simultaneously opened seven stores in Quebec in September 2013. The company planned to establish two hundred stores in Canada within a few years.[2]

Leaving the meeting, I took a few minutes to chat with my friend Mélissa. Her reintegration into the job market was going pretty well. The only downside was the schedule. She was sometimes asked to start at 5:00 a.m. When that happened, she couldn't bring her daughter to daycare, and was sometimes forced to wake the girl in the middle of the night to bring her to her mother's before continuing on her way to the store by bus. A difficult conundrum, and expensive.

"Sometimes I have no choice but to take a taxi, it forces me to work for free almost," she sighed.

She was also having a rough time with the customers. Yesterday she was scolded by a customer who was horrified to see the Halloween candies near the perfumed candles. For reasons that only a long psychoanalysis could have uncovered, the juxtaposition of candles and candies scandalized the lady, to whom it was sacrilege.

Nearby, the old Portuguese men continued to sip their coffee at McDonald's with remarkable indifference.

★

We received thirteen pallets of frozen and refrigerated products in the early afternoon. It is high time: the section is opening in two days and inaugurating empty shelves would have been embarrassing. Guess who was enlisted to haul the pallets from the warehouse to the store? The new kid, obviously. Classic. I'd like to think that my gladiator physique had something to do with it, but my girlfriend thinks that unlikely. Pencil pusher that I am, it was actually my rank that decided it. Out of evil comes good: thanks to this labour, my calves became more muscular.

By assuming the role of model employee, I had hoped to pass unnoticed. But it had the opposite effect. My bosses showed their satisfaction, sometimes in front of others. I wanted to be in their good books, of course, but I was on the way to becoming their darling. This was far from aiding relations with my dairy product colleagues, who seemed to have adopted the law of least effort. And they were not the only ones.

Because no union protected the associates, they had in a way unionized themselves. The least form of initiative was avoided like the plague and no one ever did more than the customer asked. This behaviour seemed logical and less humiliating than licking the boots of the boss who enriched himself off the sweat of your brow. I would undoubtedly see things in this light if a big, well-paying — and unionized — job didn't await me when this experience was over.

Nevertheless, I was not rejected by my work fellows. I even began to connect with Stéphanie, the dynamic manager, as well as Nancy and Karine, two women in my section. Not to mention my friend Mélissa. One sign that my integration was going well was that I began to relax. I ventured a few ribald puns and clumsy imitations of Ginette Reno, Pierre Lapointe and Bruce Willis speaking French in *Die Hard* (my pride and joy).

"What sign are you?" asked Stéphanie, good-naturedly.

"Um, Taurus."

"Of course! It shows!"

I finished the day by putting out goods in the aisles, where I received my daily dose of anger from customers. The usual, "You always change everything around here," or "we always have to look for everything" mixed with the strange titles applied to us, such as "chief," "captain" or "boss." I worked out my frustrations in the warehouse, swearing at the top of my lungs after losing a battle with a forklift that refused to lift a pallet of frozen goods, melting before my eyes.

Insignificant little annoyances, accumulating, become great frustrations.

IN MY ELEMENT

October 19, 2012

The week crawled by. I felt as though I had spent my entire life in the store. I arrived in the dark and left in the dark. The fall penetrated my existence. Things were not set to get any better.

The new schedule was announced on the billboard and I learned that I would be working evenings and weekends. I had honestly thought I would escape this kind of schedule because of my age and family situation. Wrong. I would sometimes have to get up in the middle of the night. I comforted myself by thinking that at least I wouldn't have to wake up my children to bring them to their grandmother's, as Mélissa sometimes had to do.

At the meeting this morning, the boss invited employees to visit the new Walmarts in the area. He added that our customers would no doubt be doing that out of curiousity.

"But they will come back. Why? Because of you!" he cried to the sleepy associates with a liveliness demonstrating that the lack of light was not going to have any effect on him.

Then the stretches, the rallying cry and the associates' routine work.

But routine is a very subjective concept. While I was starting to find some tasks and interactions with customers repetitive, many of my colleagues complained of having too many different things to take in. It must be admitted that a flagrant lack of coordination among management often complicated things and they ended up assigning ridiculous, even downright incomprehensible, tasks. Each section manager believed they were assigned the mission of always having the last word. "There are too many chiefs and not enough Indians around here," Stéphanie confided, a little overwhelmed by the prevailing disorganization.

Marc seemed satisfied. He sometimes brought me out of my daydreams with a kind, "Good job!"

Speaking of daydreams, it had been a while since I had had so much time for reflection. The simple and redundant work gave me ample leisure to think. At this moment, for example, I was thinking up an excuse to justify a week-long absence a short time from now. I had to go to Mexico to finish a report for *La Presse* on Mexican farmworkers who spent their summers in Quebec. I thought through pretexts that could justify my absence. Death in the family? No. It was a very suspect excuse. My older brother, Ben, that champion of high school truancy, had buried our poor grandmothers a hundred times.

Vacation in the south? That would look pretty bad, one month after being hired. And how could the expense be explained, on my salary? A friend on the point of death, after a serious accident, seemed my best option at this point. Especially since I had already gone through that, a few years ago, when a trip to Argentina with friends was transformed into a nightmare of intensive care at a hospital in Mendoza. A piece of steak stuck in the esophagus of a friend led (after questionably ethical medical practices) to the perforation of his lung. Switching from tourist to caregiver, I devoured *The Pillers of the Earth* by flashlight while cockroaches swarmed around my sick friend's bed.

Walmart requires little brain but lots of body. My feet were killing me. They had already been giving me some pain before I began working there — the unfortunate consequence of an aborted attempt to imitate fashionable people by taking up jogging. But now the pain was getting worse every day. The few hours of sleep I got between shifts weren't enough to give me relief.

My painful feet happily did not prevent me from rushing across the mall every morning break to get a café au lait. It was often one of the rare, if not the only, comfort of my workday. The waitress at the stand now started preparing as soon as she saw me coming and when she handed me my coffee, I had exactly eight minutes left in my break. I quickly returned to the job, swallowing the hot drink like someone dying of thirst in the desert. I don't remember counting the minutes like this since high school, in June.

After the break, Caroline took a few seconds to ask me if I liked my job so far.

"You seem in your element, eh?"

My element. People keep saying this to me. Did I really seem like a fish in water? I am not aware of having any particular vocation for frozen goods. Anyway.

"Yes, everything is going well, people are very nice to me."

"I like the job," I answered her without really lying.

"In any case, if there is anything and if you have problems with any-one, come see me whenever you like," added Caroline, before turning the corner at the end of the aisle.

Katia, my boss at *La Presse*, thinks that I am taking my new job too seriously, that I am even in danger of forgetting why I became an associate. I hardly ever think about my story anymore. I think about my pallets, my deliveries, my rotations, my over and my facing. I think Walmart. Katia begged me to put more effort into thinking as a journalist instead of an expert in dairy products.

I had hardly finished with Caroline when Rebecca, a young cashier, grabbed my arm, "Are you busy?"

She seemed in shock, her speech disjointed. "I hung on … or he would have run away!" The "he" in question was a thief who had been caught a few minutes earlier. "He" had been brought to the security agent's office and an employee had to stand watch while the agent wrote up his report. Three guesses who was stuck there. Yes: me. I couldn't say no to Rebecca. I found myself seated in the tiny office — windowless like all the other offices — in front of the captured thief.

He identified himself. A resident of the neighbourhood, a frail 60-year-old with a thin moustache and glasses on the end of his nose. The man was horrified. He grabbed his head in his hands and sobbed several times. The scene was poignant. The seconds ticked by like hours and I didn't know where to look, avoiding the supplicating eyes of the thief who counted on me to reason with his unrelenting jailor. The latter was taking his sweet time. The security agent dug into the suspect's bag to describe his spoils in detail. A pair of boots, a razor, razor blades, socks. Total value about $200. No one was curious about the motive. Meeting basic needs (socks, razor blades)? A fit of kleptomania? Only one thing was important: the police were on their way.

The business with the thief ended as abruptly as it had started. I went back to my frozen goods. For the past several days, shipments had arrived mid-afternoon. I thus had to do overtime to put them all on the shelves. Most associates rejoiced when they were given overtime. We were paid time and a half. I, forced to cancel my son's swimming lessons once again, did not. Swimming lessons are deadly dull, but I think of them as part of the fatherhood contract.

The rest of the day was normal. I endured the bottleneck at the lift and the logistical nightmare of manoeuvering around the store without causing an accident. While a handful of us toiled to set out half a dozen pallets, others twiddled their thumbs in the grocery section. Meanwhile, the bosses talked amongst themselves in the midst of the employees, never lifting a finger. Despite this disorganization, which made me grumble, the frozen and refrigerated sections took shape.

I left the store with a feeling of accomplishment. Before leaving, Stéphanie told me to come in later the next day as I would again finish later. This was welcome, I needed sleep. I was visibly losing weight. Though that wasn't a bad thing. On the time stamp, a note had been left for the employees: "The Wii is on supersale for $129."

THE WISE ELDER

October 20, 2012

As I parked my car in the parking lot at the store, the last of the partiers headed home to sleep. It had been ages since I had gotten up this early to work on a Saturday. Fernando, half awake, rubbed his eyes behind the customer service desk. As soon as I saw him, the refrain of his horrible morning song began to replay in my head.

"Hey, I just met you/And this is crazy/But here's my number/So call me maybe"

Many young employees were already at work in the store. I recognized some faces from the group interview last month. Hey, they had even hired Léo, the guy who had slumped in his chair and openly admitted wanting to work at Walmart because all of his friends worked there. I suddenly felt terribly old, realizing with horror that, when I had been their age, I had looked on the 35-year-old men who still worked in a supermarket with contempt. Now I was the pathetic old man.

Léo was 17 and was studying to be an ambulance technician at CEGEP. His whole life lay before him. He choked when I asked him if he envisaged a career at Walmart. "No way," he burst out, before catching himself politely, not wanting to offend me. He and the other young people used the formal "you"[3] despite my repeated attempts to be addressed informally. This mark of respect permanently reminded me that I was no longer one of them.

There are two types of employees at Walmart. Those who work full time, often older; and those who work part time, mostly students. The latter are just passing through and are given few responsibilities. And because they plan to leave, they are not too worried about the management. The majority of the weekend team were young and they didn't exactly kill themselves working. They all seemed tired, defeated, depressed; as if the end of the world were about to take place, and the Maya weren't way off base after all. Was I just as sluggish at their age? Probably, and the fact that I don't think so is just another sign of age.

For reasons I didn't immediately understand, these young people came up to me one after another to ask me what to do, though I had no more seniority than they did. I thought it must be the beard and the crow's feet. Later, Marc explained that because of my experience, he was entrusting me with training, monitoring and managing the young people in his absence. He had spread the word. My salary? It stayed the same. The only advantage was that time went more quickly handling small juvenile problems and, as a bonus, it earned my bosses' trust.

Of those who knew who I was, that is. In an aisle, I ran into the big boss of the store, François. His gaze wandered down to my badge before he greeted me.

"Ah … Hugo. I had forgotten your name."

(Believe me, my friend, you are going to remember it one day.)

THIEF OF TIME

October 21, 2012

I finished my first night shift. A completely different fauna stalks the aisles; workers doing their shopping after their job. It fell on me, as the only "full-timer," to supervise the younger people. I met Marianne, with whom I had been teamed up during the hiring interview, the one who wanted to become a police officer. The shy girl of the first day was in fact not so timid. She squabbled and flirted with the handsome Léo, the frozen goods Casanova. I always had a small group in tow when I moved around. Sometimes four to carry a half-dozen cases of milk. No one was killing themselves at work today. It gave me the chance to ham it up with my fellows. My old classic, "Would you like me T'aid you," said to a customer while brandishing a box of Tide always went over well.

As we giggled in the frozen goods aisle, a customer tapped her food behind us, as though to make us feel guilty for whistling too loudly while working. (Yes, yes, madame, let's be calm, here we go, I will show you where to find the coffee. There it is, there, beneath the giant, six-foot sign on which you can read "COFFEE." And have a nice day, come back to see us again. And, please, don't lose that magnificent smile; that is my real salary.)

A little further away, two customers in their 50s were opening a bag of crackers and helping themselves. No reaction when they saw me, quite the opposite.

"I always taste new products. When I like it, I buy it and when I don't like it, I leave the bag on the shelf. Would you like some?" one of them offered, holding out the bag and spitting bits of cracker onto my dirty pants.

Saved by the bell! It was almost 9:00 p.m., closing time. Because I still had a break, I waited for the last client to leave before buying a chocolate milk and going to drink it in the break room. A young cashier accosted me.

"You are not supposed to buy that here!" she barked.

"Why not? I'm on break."

"Yes, but you haven't punched out yet and that is stealing time," continued the vigilant colleague.

Attempting to keep my cool, I explained that it would be ridiculous to walk all the way across the vast store to punch out, come back to pay for my purchase, and then go all the way back to the break room. All the more so because the cashes were closing at that very moment.

"It's policy, sorry," she snapped.

I couldn't care less about house policy. I paid at a cash that was still open.

"I have no choice but to report you to a manager," said the irritated young colleague, eying my badge.

A few minutes before 10:00 p.m., the employees were called to the cash. Another meeting, improvised. A boss summarized the day's sales. She put the decrease in revenues down to the recent opening of other stores in the area. Finally, she announced the presence of an "honoured guest" among us, none other than the big boss of the store, standing discreetly behind us.

In the absence of anything particularly exciting to say, he reminded associates not to leave shoe marks on the walls of the warehouse. For the millionth time, he brought up the reopening of the store as a supercentre, happening in a few days.

"It's going to be the biggest attraction in town," he promised. Everyone was invited to a big party to mark the occasion, at 6:45 a.m. Several associates giggled discreetly.

"It's going to be fun, there will be lots of great people," he continued, obviously looking forward to it.

At home, I left the flyer announcing the opening on the kitchen table. My partner jokingly exclaimed, "Wow, it's really the talk of the town!"

8

DIARY OF AN ASSOCIATE II

THE SUPERCENTRE

October 24, 2012

Surreal. The adjective is perhaps overused, but I can't find any better way of describing the famous supercentre "inauguration" party at 6:45 this morning. I couldn't miss it, obviously, even though my shift only began at 8:00 a.m. Not from any obligation, but because my mission is to provide you with the best information possible, regardless of the risk to my mental health. Arriving, I heard the clamour of a crowd amassed in a corner of the store. From afar I could make out my colleagues in the company of illustrious unknowns dressed to the nines. As I approached, I realized that they were snaking through the aisles.

The loudspeakers spat out Latino music. Associates paraded by, brandishing signs bearing the names of countries, no doubt to illustrate the global reach of the company. It might have been an imitation of the opening ceremony of the Olympic Games: the name of each country was announced by a MC perched on a stage decorated with balloons. "South Africa! Australia! China!" Each greeted with a volley of applause.

François, our esteemed boss, proudly presented the clutch of dignitaries who honoured us with their presence. Managers and guests followed one after another at the podium. In a paroxysm of joy after seven months of renovations, François thanked his faithful assistants, and then invited an associate from the store up to sing. The young employee belted out a Christian gospel as though she were in the finals of *La voix*.[1] Associates clapped to encourage her. The festivities continued with a video introducing the store's bosses, with "Eye of the Tiger" as background music. Applause and strident cries varied depending on the executive on the screen, as though it were a popularity contest.

Caroline then took the floor. Her speech rang true and was very moving, which, in the circumstances, was no mean feat. She spoke of the people who motivated her to come to work every morning: the Saint-Léonard associates. She awarded stars to those who, in her opinion, had distinguished themselves by their leadership over the past months. My manager Stéphanie received one. A well-deserved honour. She is strong, valiant and even calls in to the store when she is on holiday to make sure the milk orders have been placed.

The distribution of stars concluded with another musical presentation, this time by an associate from the Point-aux-Trembles store, discovered by one of our bosses during a visit to our colleagues in the east of the island. The young woman walked shyly to the microphone, the public was uncertain, but applause burst out at the first notes of "Someone Like You," by the British singer Adele. Some in the audience furtively wiped away a few tears.

It was almost 8:00 a.m. The dignitaries had not stopped parading to the microphone to congratulate each other on their leadership (the word of the day). My favourite was the one who made an unintended pun, hailing the end of the construction, whose path had been strewn with "jobs."[2] After each speech, Jasmin, the manager who had organized the celebration, energetically clapped his hands to start others off, like an enthusiastic MC.

Three minutes before the store opened, the associates had the choice of gulping down a coffee or a croissant. A singer-songwriter had been hired for the occasion to strum his guitar on stage. He had adapted the words of a local classic, *La rue principale* (Main Street) by the Colocs, to give it a Walmart flavour: *Ça va donc ben mal su'a rue Principale, depuis qu'y ont construit le Supercentre!* (Main Street is doing really badly since a Supercentre was built there). Frontman Dédé Fortin must be spinning in his grave.

The jubilant crowd moved towards the door to greet the first customers, lined up outside. The latter were less interested in the inauguration of the supercentre than the bargains. They entered to thundering applause and cries of joy from the associates. The new arrivals tried to force their way through the jubilant crowd, some going so far as to swear or heave great sighs of exasperation at having to get around these human barriers.

In one corner, customers were grabbing discount bags of rice with near violence. One of them quickly loaded twenty of them into his cart before heading for the cash. The others awarded him a murderous glare. A similar scene was unfolding a little further along, this time around a pallet of soft drinks (six bottles for $3.49). It was 8:05 a.m. and the store was bursting at the seams. There was not a single shopping cart left at the front of the store; they were all in the aisles, where they and the people pushing them formed monstrous traffic jams. The smiles of the employees contrasted with the customers, who bore the intent look of bargain hunters. The party nevertheless spread throughout the store. Customers and associates formed a frenzied sarabande overflowing into all the aisles. Laughing, swearing, shoving, running, grabbing things. A total carnival.

In front of the dairy products, an idiot complained, "It's not even true that it's cheaper here than elsewhere!"

Near the door to the warehouse, a herd of customers threatened to stampede me. "Rice! Rice! Rice!" they chanted, clearly furious. The rice on sale disappeared as quickly as tickets for a Madonna concert, and these clients seemed determined to hold a sit-in until the next delivery. "We want rice and you employees are standing in front of the door clapping!" railed one lady.

"Um, it is the official opening and …"

"Rice! Rice! Rice!" the mob of customers interrupted me.

Pushing open the doors to the warehouse, I heaved a deep sigh of discouragement, or relief, I was not exactly sure which. It was easy to identify the new associates by their white faces. The older ones, on the other hand, had the detached air of people who have been around the block. Welcome to Walmart Saint-Léonard, where the grotesque fuels the economy.

The old Portuguese men, imperturbable as ever, sip their coffee at McDonald's as though this circus had been staged for their entertainment.

THE MILK JUG

October 26, 2012

It is no joke starting a shift at 5:00 a.m. Maybe I should console myself by thinking of the situation of my still less enviable colleagues. Nancy has to get up at 3:00 a.m. to get to work because of the limitations of public transport. Life produces strange injustices. The poorer you are, the further you live from a metro station and the more you suffer from the mediocrity of Montreal's public transit system. Potholes and traffic jams are the problems of the affluent. Perhaps this explains why they are discussed so much in the media. Just saying.

The brash neon lights of the store struck a violent contrast to the darkness outside. I had to rub my eyes before I could see people toiling in a vast workyard of pallets. The night team was at work. With no customers, pallets were strewn across the floor. My day began with a catastrophe that added to the mess. I overturned a pallet of milk while climbing into the lift.

I had neglected to secure the goods with plastic wrap, so a row of six crates of four-litre milk cartons cascaded down like a house of cards.

I watched the scene in super slow motion, like a bad film.

"Noooooooooooo!"

I told myself that this blunder would mark, with a deafening crash, the end of my career at Walmart. Many of the cartons burst on impact, and the steel floor of the lift was covered in an opaque white lake. But, in a flash, a colleague I had never seen before appeared, armed with a mop and aided by another person around my mother's age. The two quickly helped me clean up the floor and milk-splattered walls. Other colleagues hurried over, as though everyone wanted to save me from getting into trouble. When a boss finally showed up in the warehouse, all trace of the damage had disappeared.

The rest of the day went by without incident, except for a client outraged by the lack of brown beans and liquor on sale.

"Your slogan should be, 'Walmart, out of everything,' fuck!" he said, incensed. I must have been tired because I found this very funny.

PLASTERED

Saturday, October 27, 2012, 6:00 a.m.

The evening was a little too sodden, the night short; I was still working off my wine. As soon as I set foot in the store, an associate accosted me. She was someone who always spoke to me as though I were director of the store. She must have felt that I exuded a natural authority (unfortunately, at the moment I was mostly exuding the fumes of alcohol). Seized with an irrepressible and recurrent need to tell on others, she reported on her colleagues one after another for various behaviours she deemed reprehensible.

"I don't want to be a snitch, but Maurice left the hamburger meat in a cart outside the refrigerator for a long time ..."

It was like racists who begin their hate speech with, "I am not a racist, but ..." It made my stomach churn, though admittedly very little would have done so in my condition. I didn't have the strength to tell her she was knocking on the wrong door. I dodged the issue with, "Okay, leave it with me, I'll see about it."

If anyone got salmonella poisoning sometime in the fall of 2012, after buying bad ground beef at the Saint-Léonard store, I beg their pardon.

Having shaken off this annoying person, I dragged my carcass over to my section, where many very (far too) physical tasks were entrusted to me. It's strange. Sometimes we were six twiddling our thumbs on weekday evenings, while on Saturday, a very busy day, we were only four on the job. The word busy is euphemistic. No less than fifty people were tapping their feet outside the store, waiting for it to open. Five minutes later, there must have been a hundred people scouring the aisles.

By afternoon, it was pointless to try to bring pallets onto the floor.

Customers were everywhere. The shelves were ransacked, particularly the new dairy and fruit and vegetable shelves. I witnessed episodes of grocery cart road rage; the lines at the cash were endless. True to habit, Walmart enjoyed turbulent prosperity.

Ah! I forgot. I finally received the card supposedly giving me a 10 percent discount in all the Walmart stores in the world. A privilege.

A FRIGHT

October 30, 2012

"I'mmmm dreaming of a whhhittte Christmas," the store radio crooned langorously. Tomorrow is Halloween and the sounds of Christmas are already in the air. But, for the moment, it is the ghosting hour and one of my old nightmares has come back to haunt me: the modules.

Even though the damn exercises on prehistoric computers were over, for a few days, a young woman from human resources had been running after me to do a final evaluation. She apologized. "I know you are really busy and that it's a waste of time but it's required and it is the only thing left to complete your file." I had to read over the basic rules of the store, and then initial each item to confirm that I understood.

"If a customer is not satisfied, what would you do?"

"I would tell them to fuck off and go do their shopping at Metro!"

The human resources person blushed.

"I know that it is annoying, but it will be finished after this."

The exercise was mercifully soon over. Returning to my aisle, I heard a strong and virile voice shouting, "Hugo Meunier!" I turned to see who was calling me in such a tone.

Damn! My boss, Marc, flanked by the boss of the grocery section, Claudine, and the big boss, François.

"Your name is Hugo Meunier?" repeated Marc.

The small group closed ranks around me. There was no way out. I froze. Shit. Think quickly! But there was nothing to do. If I were unmasked, I would not be able to deny my identity or pretend there was a mistake about who I was. I would have no choice but to confess that I was a journalist and leave the store guiltily, eyes trained upon the floor. In any case, they couldn't execute me or beat me up in a secret dungeon.

Marc ended the suspense by handing me my card. The one that supposedly gave me a 10 percent discount in all Walmarts in the world.

"Look, I found this on the floor over there, don't lose it!"

The trio of executives continued on its way down the aisle as though nothing had happened. They had no idea how relieved I was.

With uncustomary zeal, I spontaneously offered to help a customer in order to put the fright behind me. I recognized her. A harpy who came almost every day to dump her overflow of rage onto one of the associates.

"You never have anything here. It's the only Walmart I know where you can never find anything!"

This will not stop her from coming back the next day, and the day after that. Another customer, a conspiracy theorist, buttonholed me next to talk about the Machiavellian United States, which, according to reliable sources, cleans its meat with a product laced with arsenic. He clarified that he had read this on "the internets."

Some day, it would be worth studying the therapeutic function Walmart plays.

The day was coming to a close when the Halloween monsters gave way to the holiday spirit. A lady asked for my help grabbing a container of lemon yogurt from a distant shelf. The small basket attached to the handlebars of her motorized cart was filled to the brim. Many clients did their shopping in motorized wheelchairs supplied by the company. She put the yogurt at her feet and asked me where the canned peaches could be found. I went to find her a few varieties. Her eyes lit up.

"Wow! I can spoil my daughter. She has MS and loves canned peaches. I can't wait to see her face," she said happily, rolling towards the check out.

Happiness can be canned.

MY LIFE'S SHIT

November 1, 2012

I don't like Acadian singer Lisa LeBlanc's new hit. The melody and words are deadly dull. But today I had the chorus stuck in my head, because really, "ma vie, c'est d'la marde (my life's shit)." I felt like a pariah. I had been dreading this day for a long time. I still had to figure out a cover story for my week-long absence to go do a story in Mexico. I wanted to get it over with. That is why I got to work early, before my shift started. I found Marc, for once alone in his office. I screwed up my courage.

"Boss, my mother-in-law had a stroke. She is in the hospital and it is not looking good. The problem is that she lives in western Canada. I have to go with the kids and we're leaving on Saturday after my shift. I'm really sorry for leaving you in the lurch."

Marc gazed at me with his piercing blue eyes. His face showed compassion.

"Don't feel badly. That kind of thing is outside our control."

He stretched out his arm to take a look at the schedule, ex-ing out my shifts and thinking through new scenarios. He simply wanted to ensure that my absences were covered by reliable, regular associates. In a flash, my absence was accepted. All it would cost me was a mother-in-law. But my boss' kindness made the lie painful. My double life was getting me down. I felt low.

The shortage of $1-margarine cut short my self-flagellation. Suddenly questions were flying from all sides about this damn margarine on sale.

"We don't have any left, madame. I'm sorry."

"Sorry sir, the product has run out."

No surprise that the margarine had disappeared. Customers could take as many as they wanted. Sniffing out the deal of the century, they grabbed dozens of containers of margarine; you'd think a war had just been declared. I smiled picturing the cupboards where they store their bargain reserves, in anticipation of the end of the world or an electoral victory by Quebec solidaire.

I offered up limp apologies with the air of a beaten dog, which, given the mood I was in, must have been convincing.

"I am very sorry, sir, the product has run out."

The customers seethed. One woman fixed me with a contemptuous glare for ten very long seconds. If looks could kill, I would have been found bleeding beneath my pallet of eggs.

"That's it!" she finally exploded. "I am going to do my grocery shopping elsewhere. It's always the same thing, you never have anything!"

"I am sorry, madame, but you know, it's not my fault."

"You all say that! It's never your fault!" she cut in, before disappearing down the aisle, no doubt proud to have shared what was on her mind.

When I think of the scandals exposed by the Charbonneau Commission since the beginning of the week, the drama of the margarine shortage at the Saint-Léonard Walmart seems relative. But the customer is always the boss, right? At least there are customers who do not piss me off. The old Portuguese men, as zen as ever; or the weirdo straight out of the 1980s with his leather shirt and smoked glasses, who spends his days talking to himself without ever buying anything.

Before I left, Marc came to see me. He wanted to make sure I was okay, asking me for fresh news of my mother-in-law, still sympathizing. Sigh.

I am no better than the worst of the customers or the most warped manager.

THE TWELVE LABOURS OF THE ASSOCIATE

November 2, 2012

A little before 5:00 a.m., I threw myself out of bed. I had aged prematurely. My feet hadn't forgiven me for what I'd made them endure. They made me suffer. Terribly. I could hardly walk and most of the muscles in my body were seized up with pain. Nevertheless, thirty minutes later, I arrived at work. Maurice, the perpetually sweaty night worker, opened the door to Walmart. True to habit, he greeted me with a joke and excitedly awaited my response. There wasn't any. He seemed a little disappointed and changed the subject to dispell the awkwardness. It's not my fault his jokes always fall flat.

I started my day by inspecting the refrigerators. Two pallets of yogurt had been delivered during the night. There was still enough milk on the shelves, except for the shelf of red four-litre bags, which was entirely empty. I took note. The freezer was a mess. Overflowing stock piled every which way from the back wall to the heavy aluminum door. The muffled sound of this door and the violence of -18 degrees Celcius on my barely awakened body will certainly haunt me to the end of my days.

I pulled a first pallet of cheese from the refrigerated warehouse to restock the shelves. It weighed a ton. Once inside the store, it had to be towed to the cheese aisle. The customers weren't there yet, so we could spread ourselves out, but I still didn't have time to loiter. The products cannot stay out of refrigeration for very long. I got to work, alone in my section. The cheese strings, Tropicana juice, Jell-O on sale, margarine and yogurt almost all fit onto the shelves. The uninitiated have no idea of the pleasure of fitting the contents of an entire pallet onto shelves. I would not have to haul it back half-empty to the warehouse and cram it in with the dexterity of a Tetris champion. I brought the second pallet. Yogurt, a little juice. No margarine or Fruitopia. This worried me. The margarine and Fruitopia juice were on sale; I didn't want to relive yesterday's scoldings.

It was 7:00 a.m. Marc appeared at the end of the aisle, a large coffee in his hand. The bastard. I don't know what stopped me from asking him for a sip. My boss, not a boss for nothing, had noticed that the frozen goods shelves were as empty as Antarctic beaches. My new mission: fill this void. I clutched my jacket and ventured into the freezer. Unsurprisingly, Marc wanted to feature the pizzas on special. The boss specified that there were many boxes in storage. And where were those lovely boxes? On the last pallet, stuck at the very back of the freezer. I would have to pull out the five pallets that blocked the pizza pallet, drag it out and place it on the floor and then put the other five back into the freezer before they thawed.

It was not yet 8:00 a.m. when two of the five pallets I had to pull out collapsed when I tugged on them. My suspicions naturally settled on the teenagers working the evening shift, who must have set them up too quickly. The day before I hadn't seen my valiant 17-year-old comrade in the evening. No doubt he was off having fun with the other youngsters. I had to fight down a furious desire to tell on them. When they idle, I work for two.

On the intercom, the meeting was announced. Fuck! No time this morning for the Walmart chant and cheering. With difficulty, I finished getting my pizza pallet out, though not without causing a significant traffic jam in the corridors.

"It won't be long, it won't be long, my pallets will be back in the freezer in no time."

My colleagues didn't seem to share my sense of urgency. On the contrary, they seemed rather pleased to take a breather while I broke my back hauling like an ox. My suffering gave Gaétanne a pretext to talk to Francine about her back strain.

"I am 55 years old. I have passed the age when I can get down on all fours in the trailer to haul pallets," said the beddings employee, whose family doctor had prescribed light work. But, she said, "Light work doesn't exist here …"

Back in the store, I didn't even have time to stick the blade of my knife into the plastic wrap of the first box of pizza when my name was announced, "Hugo at reception please."

Stéphanie barged onto the floor at the same time. We had just received nine pallets. We would only keep the one with the one-dollar lemonade. The rest would have to be warehoused outside in our 53-foot refrigerated trailer parked a few meters from the store.

What followed was a real Olympic trial: I had to drag the nine pallets of milk from the reception to the basement, then take the elevator to the second floor and bring them to the door of the other reception, from which the refrigerated trailer could be accessed. They were seven-foot-high loads: fifty-six crates, each containing four bags of four litres of milk. Do the math. My crimson face commanded the respect of customers, who realized that this was not the time to annoy me. By the third pallet, I lost patience. Why was I always the one slapped with these shitty jobs! Then a string of swear words. Only Eduardo, an immense guy, dared interrupt.

"That's a lot of curse words!" he remarked.

After this workout, I was starving. I went to eat. I also needed a coffee. No, two. Going to the washroom after my meal, I discovered, to my horror, a pair of men's soiled underwear behind the toilet bowl. They stank. I gave Michel, the maintenance manager, a furtive but solidarity-minded thought before fleeing back to my job in the warehouse.

Jimmy, the fruit and vegetable hiree, recently let go from the Laval store, pushed open the door to the warehouse. His face was livid and his eyes haunted, as though he had just witnessed a death.

"It's completely crazy here."

My fellows and I exchanged glances before bursting into laughter. Poor guy. It was a day like any other. Grueling, yes, but they all were.

We deserved every cent of our minimum wage.

THE SHOW MUST GO ON

November 3, 2012

Alright! One last day on the job before I leave for Mexico. Hang in there! When I arrived, the fruit and vegetable colleagues were already there; they had been hard at work since 5:00 a.m. Karine had been brooding on bitter thoughts for several days. A wind of mutiny was blowing in her section.

Speaking of mutiny, my morning conversations with Liam would surely have earned us a hundred lashes in the public square if we had been heard in high places. Liam was the first (and last) to openly say the word "union" in my presence. The term is completely taboo in the store.

"A manager already told me that everything is in place to dismantle any attempt to unionize," Liam confided.

This rumour was confirmed by a former manager I met while writing this book. The latter, who wanted to remain anonymous, was categorical: "The manager is instructed to report any mention of the word union to the administration. The word is frightening. We were told that if the union enters, the store will close."

The same manager told me that when my infiltration became known, a state of alert was triggered in her store more than an hour from Montreal and in many others across the province, it seems. Meetings were held at the top among bosses and then again with employees included. "If a journalist comes in here and asks questions, immediately report him to the administration!"

But, to return to the frozen goods. Customers began to fill the aisles. Eight o'clock already. The teenagers came to ask me what to do, for a change. I liked these teens very much, even though they were lazy. Maybe they were just smarter than I was at their age, when I broke my back for badly paying jobs, as though my future depended on it. Sébastien, who worked in the fruit and vegetable aisle, came to see me, complaining about his manager.

"Why don't you be our boss, Hugo, I think we'd like to work for you!"

Great, so now I was becoming a role model for youth. It was the only thing missing.

Suddenly, my manager Stéphanie appeared out of nowhere, in civilian clothing. "Hugo, do you have a couple of minutes? I need to talk to you!"

She took me by the arm to the human resources office. She handed me an application form.

"I am not supposed to do this, but …"

A position had opened in my department. I understood that it was destined for me. The dice were loaded.

It works the same way at *La Presse*. Somewhat as a joke, I applied a few years ago for a columnist position that was tailor-made for Patrick Lagacé. They lured him all the way to Saint Jacques street by promising him this position. The game was rigged. I unsuccessfully attempted to reshuffle the deck by promising my bosses to mow their lawns for life if they gave me the job. I should have realized that the bosses of *La Presse* were dwellers of Montreal's trendy Plateau neighbourhood, winter cyclers and summer joggers, whose homes have no lawns.

In the end, here I was, forced to apply for a full-time job at Walmart. The show must go on.

9

OPERATION SUN

In the photo, Patrice Bergeron is a dashing young man, his face confident. Far off in the background stands the store. The photo is tiny, you have to squint to recognize the people. There is a short text taken from a Radio Canada report. In journalistic jargon, it's called a bottom legend.

It says: "The Jonquière Walmart closed Friday at noon, one week ahead of schedule. This store's employees were the first in the chain to get union certification in North America."[1]

The unionization of a store in Jonquière, in 2004, caused a veritable earthquake in the world of Walmart. Writing this book without mentioning this union battle would be like making a film on the Titanic without sinking the ship. The event was important enough to figure in a Quebec history textbook,[2] sharing the limelight with René Lévesque. Patrice Bergeron showed me, not without pride, the textbook in which the struggle he had led more than ten years ago was immortalized.

This young man, who was a thorn in the giant's side for many months, is sitting at the kitchen table in his apartment on des Chutes Boulevard in Beauport, about two hundred kilometers from the store we saw in his photo. He has gained a little weight and seems more serious but appears to be just as sure of himself. Beside him is his partner Alexandra Genest. She will soon give birth to their first child. The couple formed during the union struggle. She is thus very familiar with the story that Patrice is about to tell me and that he usually only shares with people close to him. In her way, Alexandra played a role in the story.

"I handed him the lighter to burn his Walmart uniform in our protests!" she recalls, eying the future father of her child affectionately.
The anecdote makes Patrice smile.

The *belle époque*? More like the dirty epoch.

Patrice Bergeron had just turned 21 when he saw a job offer in the
local paper for the new Walmart store opening in Jonquière. The young
man from Saguenay was not great at school. He saw a career opportunity.
He had three interviews; two individual and one group, where he was
asked to sing the Walmart song. He remembers the issue of telling on
others being omnipresent in the individual interviews with several different managers. "If you caught a colleague stealing, what would you do?"

The young man's answers were satisfactory and he landed the job.
His hourly wage was $7.70, about twenty-five cents more than mini-
mum at the time. Because he was hired full-time, he was promised
a minimum of twenty-eight hours of work per week. He got a night
shift in the warehouse. His role was to unload goods from the trailers
to stock the store, which was under construction and due to open in
October 2001.

He quickly discovered that some things in his new job were not right.
For example, a manager strongly recommended that he not discuss
working conditions with other employees, especially not wages. Patrice
quickly understood why. No one seemed to have the same salary, not
even those who did exactly the same work. A detail, you may say, but
the message is clear: employees should associate with Walmart, not
each other.

Patrice began to discuss unionization with a night worker who had
contacts at the *Confédération des syndicats nationaux* (Confederation
of National Unions, or CSN). He had been working at Walmart for
several months now. To avoid trouble, the two men gave the union
a code name: Sun. The student learned a host of things about union
culture from the teacher. But they were alone. There was instant malaise
when they broached the issue with other colleagues, as though they were
trying to prove the non-existence of God in a monastery. Worse, the
code didn't fool the bosses for very long. As soon as they heard of the
night worker's ideas, they summoned him to a meeting to call him to
order. He immediately quit.

His departure was like a slap on the face to Patrice. He energetically tried to dissuade his colleague from jumping ship, but in vain.

"In the end, he passed the torch on to me," which, Patrice stressed, was no small matter. Alone, rather unprepared, the young man sought help. He got in touch with a regional union advisor of the *Fédération des travailleurs du Québec* (Federation of Workers of Quebec, or FTQ).

"We are a small group who would like to unionize," Patrice told the union advisor.

"Which store?"

"The Jonquière Walmart."

"Seriously?!"

It was a worthy cause, but the FTQ advisor knew from experience that it wouldn't be easy. How on earth could a union be established in one of the most anti-union companies in the world? At Walmart, the slightest mention of the word union caused a commotion and immediately triggered defence mechanisms. It was like shouting "Long live Bin Laden" at the customs desk of the New York airport after September 11. At Walmart a telephone line is "available to managers 24 hours a day: at the first sign of attempts at [union] organizing, they must call this number 'as quickly as possible.'"[3]

Patrice Bergeron, barely out of his teens, a lightweight from Saguenay, had undertaken mission impossible.

The Jonquière employees nevertheless had several advantages. Canadian laws were not unfavourable to them. In the United States, individuals are more or less left to themselves in their dealings with big companies. This is no longer the case in Canada, where the law stands as a reminder that if there were no brakes on the organized power of money, individual dignity and freedom would be no more than empty words. In other words, the law does not attribute freedom to companies alone. It also upholds the free association of workers. This explains why the only attempts to unionize Walmart stores — four in total — all happened in Canada. To get union certification in the country, 50 percent plus one of the employees must have initialed a membership card. In the Jonquière store, this corresponded to a hundred people.

The FTQ explained to Patrice that he had to establish a balance of power in order to be heard. He must rally employees to his cause. Two other associates felt the union tension building in the aisles. They were glad and plunged into the fray. The three men carried the union message to the different departments of the Jonquière Walmart. "We had to start taking action and see if people were interested," Patrice explained.

Even as he discreetly carried out his union activities, Patrice applied for and got a position displaying dairy products. That was when his troubles started. One week after his transfer to food, two bosses called him into an office. "Sit down," one of them ordered, while the other remained standing in front of the door with his arms crossed.

"Pat, it seems you are harassing the employees, talking about unions, I've had complaints. I no longer want you to talk about that here, or things will not go well," warned the manager.

The scenario played out again three days later. Same choreography. Two bosses, one sitting, the other standing with crossed arms in front of the door. But this time the tone was cranked up a notch.

"If you talk about the union again, you are halfway out of here."

Caught by surprise, Patrice claimed that he already had enough membership cards to get union certification. A big, fat lie. In reality, not a single card had been signed, not even his own. The blow struck the managers dumb. One of the bosses went pale, as though he had seen the ghost of Sam Walton pointing an accusing finger at him. A wave of panic overwhelmed the small administrative team, who allowed Patrice to return to work in his section as though nothing had happened. The managers followed him out of the office, their ears glued to their cell phones.

"There was total panic," Patrice said, smiling. The bluff undoubtedly changed the course of things. From that moment on, no one took Operation Sun lightly; a victory in itself, achieved without having had a single membership card signed.

Being taken seriously brought its own difficulties, however. The atmosphere deteriorated. "I was scared stiff. The bosses didn't give me an inch, they spied on me," recalled Patrice.

Only a minority of employees spontaneously joined ranks with the three union activists. Above all, employees feared the newly opened store would close. The managers happily fueled this fear. The psychological warfare was brutal. One of the three miscreants, Pierre

Martineau, cracked up. He was booed at every morning meeting; even on his birthday he was treated to this humiliation. He sometimes fled to the washrooms to cry. At 60 years old, he was destroyed. Nor did Patrice escape the harassment. A deathly silence greeted him every time he set foot in the store. His colleagues almost feared breathing the same air; as though they would be found guilty by association if they were openly friendly towards him. He became a pariah.

It was obviously impossible to recruit members within the store, where associates were shackled by fear. With FTQ advisors, Patrice decided to go meet his colleagues at their own homes. But he still had to find out where his colleagues lived. With the means available to him, Patrice undertook making a list of all Jonquière Walmart employees.

"I saw people in the breaks and subtly asked them their last names and their husbands' names. At night I used the phone book to call them. When I got the right address, I hung up."

He used another strategy, effective but unorthodox: tailing employees by car after their shift.

"My brother helped me, as well as my cousin, which helped me get membership cards signed, notably by a skirt-chaser who was very anti-union at first but didn't know how to say no to such a pretty girl."

The end justified the means, or almost.

Nine months later, Patrice had an exhaustive list of employees and their addreseses. A real feat, given staff turn over. For the United Food and Commercial Workers Canada (UFCW), whose local came on board to lend Patrice a hand, the time was ripe. A membership drive should be launched.

It was too good to be true. Exhausted by months of preparation, Patrice's crew announced it was abandoning the struggle. Misfortune never comes singly and UFCW also threw in the towel when these defections were announced. Once again Patrice found himself alone.

But Patrice Bergeron wasn't going to let himself be defeated. If he had to cross a desert to get to his goal, he would. He soon reconstituted a small union cell. Johanne Desbiens and her best friend, two cashiers, threw themselves into the fray. They gathered the missing addresses and, along with Patrice, the little team began to sign up members to the union. Signatures came in, slowly but surely. First friends from the warehouse, then some cashiers, and then lips began to loosen: associates complained about some aspects of their work, the precarity of their conditions, the difficult schedules — and the number of signatories soared. Many were afraid. At night they called Patrice at home for reassurance.

In December 2003, a first union application was filed. There was a secret vote. It failed. The blitz had brought in seventy signatures, but this was insufficient. Thirty more were needed to form a union. According to Patrice, the threat of closure triumphed over the desire to unite. Discouragement prevailed and Patrice and his friends decided to take a break and allow the dust to settle. Membership cards were valid for a year. That gave them a little time.

Fortunately, news is not always bad. A new employee soon decided to step up. The troops respected him. Enter Gaétan Plourde.

GAÉTAN PLOURDE

When Gaétan Plourde came onto the scene, the union movement had run out of steam. He gave it new life and carried it with force through to the end. Nothing predestined this man for unionism, however.

Gaétan's adventure began in the summer of 2001 with an advertisement in the Chicoutimi *Le Quotidien*. Employees were sought for a future Walmart in Jonquière. This former manager of a European framing company, which had moved its offices overseas, decided to apply. Because of his previous position, he shared the bosses' point of view.

"I was able to put myself in the employer's shoes," Plourde told me, when I met him thirteen years later in a restaurant. But, "in the framing company, the employees didn't want to form a union because they were well-paid and well-treated," he explained.

The short, bearded man with a lively eye was at first hesitant to talk. It is his name that appears on the legal files as the representative of the Jonquière Walmart employees. It is very exhausting to fight a company. A corporation like Walmart is a vast bureaucratic organization, with no scruples, no feelings, which never gets tired, operates twenty-four hours a day and exists for money alone. It is difficult for simple mortals to stand up to such machines. Gaétan Plourde was tired. He was probably sick of journalists, lawyers, lawsuits and public education campaigns. He looked at me, as if to ask, what will I get out of telling you all of this? I had put a lot of time and effort into my investigation, I had lived as an associate; maybe that was what convinced him. Who knows? In any case, in the end he opened up to me, journalist though I was.

My first question was obvious. Why would a man who has a degree in teaching and professional experience want to work on the bottom rung at Walmart?

His response was surprising: "I am familiar with Quebec and European businesses, I wanted to know how American businesses worked." Plourde nevertheless promised himself that he would end the experiment after one year. The future decided otherwise!

Gaétan had no difficulty getting hired at Walmart. He recalled being impressed by the director of Walmart during his hiring interviews. This man turned out to be an inspired speaker, passionate and jovial. His infectious energy immediately charmed Plourde.

"He told me that we work hard at Walmart but have fun. I was happy because I share this philosophy."

A video summarizing the corporate philosophy was shown to candidates during the three hiring interviews, he recalled. The rallying cry irritated many of them, including Gaétan, who saw it as a sort of indoctrination. About fifteen people actually got up and walked out of the room. Gaétan is still absolutely convinced that the company uses this rallying cry to separate the wheat from the chaff; that is, the independently minded from docile employees.

The new associates began to work the following month, to help set up the new store. In this way, Gaétan Plourde got to know the 225 brand-new soldiers of the Jonquière garrison.

"It was a golden period," he explained. "I had 225 friends at that time."

The joy of new beginnings and big inaugurations helped him pass over some annoyances, of which the damn rallying cry every morning was not the least. Gaétan, a team player, went along with the flow.

"I didn't want to be marginal, and I had wanted to work for them."

His only request, which was granted, was to be assigned to the electronics department, because he had some knowledge in this area. Well-liked by the management, he quickly became permanent.

Time passed and, two years after being hired, Gaétan was surprised to find himself still working at Walmart. It was at this time that he heard talk about the union. The rumour was that young Patrice Bergeron was discreetly orchestrating a campaign to form a union. The night workers were talking about it openly. Gaétan, a loyal employee, didn't want to get his hands dirty; moreover, the management had always seemed to him to be open to suggestions. A meeting had even been organized the previous year with the goal of improving work and quality of life at the store. Gaétan had submitted a list of grievances, nothing very serious.

But then, a short time later, a similar meeting was organized and Gaétan realized that there had been no follow-up on suggestions made the previous year. Another meeting, just as sterile, took place and the electronics associate had to face the facts: the bosses were merely executives, they had no real decision-making power. It was impossible to improve things for the employees by appealing to local management. In this way, he came to see the union as the logical choice, since shutting up was not an option for him.

Up to that point, Gaétan had only listened to conversations about the union with half an ear; now he added his two cents. He signed a membership card, given to him by two cashiers. These two had quietly continued recruiting after Patrice Bergeron had pulled back to play a less visible role. The fierce struggle against the management had singled him out. Caution demanded that he take a backseat so as not to harm the movement. He continued behind the scenes, especially by getting membership cards signed.

It was the two cashiers who recruited Gaétan into the union nucleus.

Hostilities resumed, more virulent than ever, dividing the store into two camps. On one side, discontented workers wanting to organize; on the other, ardent opponents of the union, led by several department managers. The associates of the first group hoped to obtain the right to speak for themselves by associating in a union; the second group feared store closure and unemployment, a fear fed by the managers. This polarization lasted throughout the conflict.

The bosses were dismayed to learn that Gaétan was involved in the union. Not their good Gaétan! The traitor was summoned to their office to clarify. The same scenario played out: a boss standing in front of the door with his arms crossed; the other leading the discussion, seated before the employee.

"You are prohibited to speak about unions during working hours. This is your first warning."

But the damage was done. The bosses had lost confidence in their model employee.

The application for union certification and the vote took place six months later. Again, the employees rejected the union. It was a bitter disappointment for the activists, who had poured their heart and soul into the cause, their cause. The night of the defeat, UFCW organized a press conference in its offices. The turmoil at the Jonquière Walmart was beginning to attract attention. The president delivered a rousing, inspiring speech and, by a strange twist, the defeat took on the aspect of victory.

It was no time to fold one's arms. Gaétan and his team redoubled their efforts and went back to the vote. The third time proved successful: 160 out of 200 employees had signed membership cards. In August 2004, the employees of a Walmart in the Saguenay obtained union certification. A first in the history of the multinational in North America.

There was euphoria. The drama, which had been local up to then, instantly made world news. How would Walmart react?

THE EMPIRE STRIKES BACK

The exhilaration of victory gave way to difficult days. The administration was disorganized, overwhelmed by events, but the managers, incensed, jumped into the fray and literally took control of the store.

"The harassment intensified. We criticized the management for not calming things down, but it must have suited them," Gaétan now believes.

After the union was certified, a manager had a flyer distributed to employees. The title speaks for itself: "How union organisers create problems at Walmart." This twenty-line text described the union organizer as a parasite worse than scabies. The flyer warned associates that "once they manage to infiltrate a store," organizers only seek to get membership cards signed, saying it was beneficial. But this carried a risk because, "these people can be dangerous for Walmart. Not only because of their union activities, but because they generally believe themselves to be 'above' company policies." It would not be surprising, continued the text, to see an organizer goad the management with the sole purpose of provoking disciplinary measures and thus being able to "file a complaint for unfair practices against the store."

From all appearances, the contents of this flyer were pulled from a highly confidential internal document called "A Manager's Toolbox to Remaining Union Free."[4] This document was designed to provide executives with the tools to guard against attempts to unionize at Walmart. The company always officially denied the use of this document on Canadian soil. I nevertheless got my hands on this twenty-four-page information kit.

The kit begins by reminding the management team of its strategic importance because it constitutes "our first line of defence against unionization."[5] A list of resource people to contact in Bentonville as soon as union activity occurs is included for the foot soldiers of the first line of defence. "DO NOT GIVE THESE PHONE NUMBERS TO A UNION REPRESENTATIVE OR ANYONE OUTSIDE WALMART!" it says in capital letters, with the word "not" underlined.[6] Walmart maintains that it is not anti-union but simply pro-associate.

A philosophical nuance full of finesse: "It is our position every associate can speak for him/herself without having to pay his/her hard-earned money to a union in order to be listened to and have issues resolved."[7]

In French, "associate" has two main meanings. It can mean that one owns shares in a company — not the case for all Walmart employees — or it can mean that one is a member of an association. Walmart is the association to which "associates" belong. But if, as the document indicates, "every associate can speak for himself or herself" within the company, who speaks in the name of the association; that is, in the name of everyone? The big bosses of Bentonville, of course. This is the crux of the matter. Walmart believes that it is harmful for an associate's loyalty to be divided between a union and the company. The name of all should be Walmart alone; and the associate should be the individual alone.

Within this mindset, unionization creates a business within the business; a worm within the apple. The information kit doesn't mince its words: "Unions are not a club, sorority, fraternity or social organization. They are a business, a big business, that needs to make money."[8] The kit explains that, to avoid such internal competition, it is important to take care of the troops' morale. An unhappy associate "will tend to be seduced by the beautiful promises of the organiser."[9] The document lists some tools to measure morale, including evaluations, meetings, and keeping an eye on levels of absenteeism.

The kit then tells management staff how to argue to employees that unionization is worthless. A rather unoriginal "for" and "against" list is set out:

UNIONS CANNOT:
• Guarantee higher wages
• Guarantee better benefits
• Guarantee employment
• Guarantee hours worked
• Prevent terminations
• Set job standards

UNIONS CAN:
• Collect dues, fees, fines and assessments
• Negotiate
• Strike.[10]

That said, the best way of fighting union organizers, or "salts" as they are referred to in the kit, is to not hire them: "We are under no obligation to hire an applicant who is defiant or negative. Keep looking until you find the best applicant to join our Wal-Mart family."[11]

But if such rabble-rousers slip through the net, how can they be recognized? The kit sets out a list of distinguishing signs of the union organizer (called "early warning signs"). These are divided into two categories. First, there are suspect behaviours that should sound the alarm: abnormally high absenteeism, confrontations with managers, slowdown of productivity at work, growing curiosity about social benefits and ... misuse of the toilets. The second category includes much less equivocal facts: open discussions about unions, strangers coming and spending an abnormal amount of time with associates in the parking lot, associates who have never been seen together starting to talk and "forming strange alliances."[12]

The rest of the document describes in detail the kinds of union actions that may be organized if the threat materializes; from pickets to flyering and negative publicity. Managers are told how they should act when a union is at their door: "Do tell associates the law permits the company to permanently replace them if there is a Strike. Do tell associates if a union is voted in, everything (their wages, benefits and working conditions) would go on the bargaining table. It is much like the game show LET'S MAKE A DEAL! They could get more, they could get the same, or they could get less."[13]

In their essay, Gilles Biassette and Lysiane J. Baudu evoke the existence of this mysterious document, "which describes in detail what should raise a flag for a vigilant manager if his outlet has been selected as a 'target' by unions."[14]

One thing seems obvious: Walmart is determined to fight unionization. The American human rights organization, Human Rights Watch, published a damning report on Walmart, which it accuses of violating the rights of workers to freedom of association in unions. The conclusions of the report are categorical: "Walmart has devised a comprehensive battery of sophisticated corporate institutions and practices aimed at frustrating union organizing activity."[15]

However, the tone is far more conciliatory in a guide distributed to company employees since 2003. A section entitled Our Opinion of Unions reads,

> Walmart respects the rights of its associates, including the decision to join a union or not. Associates have the recognized right to make such a decision without intimidation, coercion or influence from ANYONE AT ALL. The company is always

ready to discuss this issue or any other work-related topic with associates who wish to do so. Walmart is not against unionization. However, while a union may represent its members who work for other employers or competitors in the retail commerce industry well, Walmart believes that if its values and beliefs are applied there is no real or marked advantage to joining a union.[16]

As there is a world of difference between the official guide, which says it respects the will to unionize, and the confidential document, which suggests taking steps against unionization, let's look at the facts: in February 2005, senior management from Toronto headquarters travelled to Jonquière to announce that the store would close. It wasn't profitable enough, one of the visitors said in broken French to justify the decision.

Patrice Bergeron and Gaétan Plourde were not fooled: they were paying the price — a big one — for their flirtation with unionism. The union organizers had previously taken the threat of closure with a grain of salt. After all, who would have imagined that a brand new store, with many customers, where 225 employers worked hard and well, would be closed? With confidence in the future, they had set out the framework for the first collective agreement with the help of UFCW. The employment contract was modelled on agreements in effect at IGA and Metro supermarkets. The employees asked for forty-hour weeks for full-time employees, paid sick leave, pay raises and, most of all, they wanted to be able to speak as a group. They weren't asking for the moon, in Patrice Bergeron's view. But it was too much for the retail giant.

News of the closure filtered out over two days to the employees, who were summoned into a room in small groups.

The atmosphere was tense when Gaétan was present. The human resources director spoke: "The store is less and less profitable. It will be closed," he dropped, like the fall of a guillotine. Some managers immediately burst into tears.

"It's unacceptable!" protested Gaétan.

The executive didn't have time to open his mouth before the managers shot back, "It's your fault, asshole, it's because of the union!"

Walmart always argued fiercely that the union had nothing to do with the closure.

It was hell for Gaétan Plourde. A hostile welcoming committee awaited him in front of the store the next morning. Night workers and several managers.

"Are you happy, Gaétan! You made us lose our jobs!" colleagues called to him, encouraged by applause.

The intimidation continued every day. The managers had given the word to pass the electronics department as often as possible. When Gaétan was alone, they insulted him.

"It really smells of shit over here!"

On top of the insults were death threats, Gaétan told me. It was Patrice Bergeron who warned him, "I heard rumours. It seems some people want to take care of you."

Whether or not there was any basis to it, the threat scared the union activist.

His ordeal ended on April 29, 2005, when the doors were officially closed. After the closure, to twist the blade in the wound, the employees — unionized or not — had to dismantle the store. Great atmosphere! To the employees, overwhelmed by the events, this final task seemed like a sadistic punishment and a warning for the future.

However, Gaétan's struggle was not over. It continued outside the store for ten long years. Ten years of legal recourse and negotiations. Ten years devoted to trying to have it recognized that closing the store had contravened the law. Despite the length of the ordeal, he never thought of abandonning it.

"You don't jump ship when it is sinking. I knew we had the means to defend ourselves in Quebec. I kept thinking, 'Who do you think you are, Walmart, to come here and dictate your laws to us?'"

When the Supreme Court ruled in their favour in 2014, Gaétan Plourde felt as though he were emerging from a long nightmare.

"The highest court in the land said I was right. I could hold my head up at last — though no higher than my five feet, five inches," he laughed.

In his view, popular education should be carried out before there is any renewed attempt to unionize Walmart. The perpetually full parking lots at Walmart stores never fail to remind him of this.

"There is a lack of solidarity from consumers. People should ask themselves questions. At one point, I began hating my own people, because they were not behind me."

Having become about as popular as a leper in the area, Patrice packed his bags and moved to Quebec City after the store closed. He now works as an aide to people with intellectual disabilities, where he dreams of becoming a union advisor. Before pulling his life back together, he fell into alcoholism, depression and came within a hair of dying in a car accident. A long, traumatizing descent into hell. Does he regret having gotten involved in the fight? No, he answered immediately.

"I still kicked American ass."

DIARY OF AN ASSOCIATE III

MEXICAN DETOUR

November 9, 2012

"We are the power," read the t-shirts of employees of a Walmart store situated almost in the centre of Mexico City. In Mexico to do a report on farm workers, I took the opportunity to visit Walmart. Walmart's adventure in Mexio started at the beginning of the 1990s, around the same time the giant set up shop in Canada. These two neighbours of the United States were obvious choices for Walmart when the the three countries signed the free trade agreement.

The chain was successfully established in Mexico. Walmart is now the biggest private employer in the country, with around 250,000 workers. Nearly 20 percent of all Walmart stores in the world are located in Mexico. The American brand is now part of the landscape and people in the country affectionately call it Walmex.

That said, the Mexican conquest was not all smooth sailing. Several controversies rocked the company. The biggest scandal was exposed by the *New York Times* in April 2012.[1] The daily revealed that Walmart's head officers in Mexico had spent nearly $30 million in bribes between 2002 and 2005 to accelerate the giant's expansion. Discovering this in 2005, Walmart had wanted to deal with these malpractices discreetly and keep the matter quiet. The alleged acts, which seemed to have involved politicians and heads of the Mexican branch of the company, led to a huge investigation.

In the same year, 2005, the opening of a store in Teotihuacan, right in the middle of an important archeological site, sparked an unprecedented national controversy. But the numerous protests, blockades, petitions and even hunger strikes were unable to impede the opening of the store near a pre-Columbian city.

"Some saw this as a desecration of a sacred site, which would disturb the peace of Quetzalcoatl, the serpent god."[2] Hundreds of people nevertheless amassed in front of the doors on opening day. But, "the connection between the cash registers and Bentonville headquarters was down," making transactions impossible.[3] How not to see this failure as a "sign that the gods were angry?"[4]

Popular outcry against the opening of a Walmart on the Mayan site of Tulum also failed. The resistance was energetic and boisterous, but the proverbial silent majority did not frown on the opening of these stores, which it associated with modernity and, above all, job opportunities.

In all, 350 associates run the Mexican store I entered in Mexico City. The store was spacious, shiny and new, in contrast to the slightly seedy appearance of the Saint-Léonard store. The customers seemed much better off than in Montreal, the goods were adapted to the local culture, but the building appeared to be cast in the same mold as every other Walmart in the world. This replica of the American formula has been a cause for concern within the company. "In Mexico, because they don't have a car, customers — especially those interested in going to discount stores — use public transit. After shopping, they have to carry their overflowing bags across the deserted parking lots to get to the bus stop. This encourages them to return to their old habit of shopping in small neighbourhood stores."[5]

I made my discovery trip to the Walmart store with the help of my translator Aurélie, a French woman who had lived in Mexico City for almost twenty years. I fabricated a character for myself: a Canadian colleague who wanted to begin his life anew in Mexico with his girlfriend (Aurélie) and was considering a job transfer.

My investigation began with Erika, who was facing a shelf of tinned goods when I approached her. A teenager with long, jet-black hair and magnificent almond eyes, she had just been hired. She liked working here, she told me, even though she only earned 12 pesos an hour, the equivalent of $1 CDN. When her three-month probation period came to a close, her salary would barely rise. Erika confirmed that the employees met every morning at 8:00 a.m. for the rallying cry and the solemn announcement of the previous day's financial results by section.

A little further in, I met Victor, stocking peppers in the fruit and vegetable section. He wore himself out in this aisle six days a week. A difficult job, which he also said he liked. He earned 3,500 pesos per month, about $290 CDN.

I noticed with astonishment that the store was not crowded. In fact, I saw more associates than customers. To me, this was a complete reversal. For Victor, it was normal. In a country where the average income is half of ours, Walmart is not accessible to the masses. In the store, the loudspeakers reverberated with American hits; security agents armed with shotguns patrolled the store on the look-out.

In another aisle, Isabelle was on her knees stocking a shelf with lightbulbs. She had been working there for three years. She seemed exhausted, her features drawn. Shadows under her eyes, her look bleak. She railed against some of her colleagues, whom she accused of loitering on the job.

"It forces me to work twice as much!"

This recrimination sounded familiar; it erased the 3,725 kilometers separating our two stores. I felt in solidarity with this associate. She earned 3,000 pesos per month, the equivalent of $250 CDN, and had never heard of my employee card, which is supposed to give a 10 percent discount in all Walmarts in the world. And the customers?

"We can't say anything against them," the employee immediately replied, on her guard. "They are our bosses."

A little further on, Javier was working in the soft drinks section. Behind him, boxes of condoms are hanging on shelves where bottles of tequila are sold. The boss of this store had foresight! Javier worked for the state as a civil servant for twenty years, before being laid off and landing here.

"It is not ideal, but I have a family to feed," he explained.

He also earned 3,000 pesos per month. In his view, there was no need to be ashamed of working at Walmart; it was a job like any other. Martin, a driver hired the day before, had voiced a totally different opinion: Walmart was the worst job possible and its bosses had terrible reputations. Javier hadn't heard of my card that gives a 10 percent discount on all merchandise either.

I met Carolina, the human resources manager, in her cramped and windowless office on the second floor of the huge store. A framed photo of Sam Walton, with his reassuring face, hung on the wall behind her. She presented a long list of jobs available in the store: salesman, deputy-head, head, manager. There was certainly a place for me in the store, she assured me. Just ask my employer to send a transfer request and it was done. At Canadian salary levels, above market, she added, which seems incredible to me. She didn't believe language would be a barrier. I had experience and, she said, I wouldn't need to speak to carry out the work expected of me. The message was clear. They would need me for my arms, not my grey cells. Nevertheless, my knowledge of English and French would be a plus for interacting with the many foreign customers at this Walmart. The only downside: I would have to shave my beard, which was prohibited here. Only mustaches were allowed. The Eldorado of hipsters, great!

The base salary for Mexican workers was 3,000 pesos per month, or $250. It was a paltry wage, clearly insufficient to survive in the capital, where the cost of living has been rising as the gap widens between rich and poor.

"And your customers? They treat you well, Carolina?"

"The customers are like everywhere else I imagine," said the employee in a telling tone.

Carolina scribbled down the address and names of resource people to give to my employer. According to her, I had a good chance of starting soon, at the beginning of the holiday season.

Leaving the human resources office, I shuddered in passing a work station equipped with old computers used for the training modules that had driven me crazy. A little further, I saw a bulletin board with the Walmart three commandments in Spanish: respect for the individual, service to customers and striving for excellence.

Before leaving, I conducted a final experiment. I grabbed a few trinkets and took out my employee card to get my 10 percent discount at the cash. The cashier took it, examined it from all angles inquiringly, then returned it to me, shaking her head from right to left. I put the useless bit of plastic back into my pocket and left the air-conditioned store under the blank stare of the security guards, armed to the teeth.

A PROMOTION

November 12, 2012

It was freezing this morning. The dry wind whipping my face didn't help. I had returned from Mexico with whitish skin. I couldn't return from my trip with a tan because everyone thinks I have been at the bedside of my dying mother-in-law in western Canada. I had thus fastidiously lathered on the suntan lotion every day, like a hypochondriac convinced that the sun's rays exist only to give him skin cancer.

My day began like all others. With the sales figures mass. Sales stopped at $171,000 yesterday, we learned from Réal, returned this morning from a week's vacation. He has artfully groomed hair and a closely shaven face. With my two-month beard, I must haved looked to him like a primate that has let itself go; he already made a more or less subtle monkey reference to me a few weeks ago.

After that, we received savings coupons, as is customary before holidays. Three coupons entitling the bearer to a 20 percent reduction. The employees use them for almost all their holiday shopping. Nothing ventured, nothing gained, as they say.

Decorations had been hung from the ceiling of the break room. DVDs of the store inauguration were being sold at $5 a piece to fund the Christmas party. No question of putting myself through that torment again, it would be better to binge-watch the first five hundred episodes of Big Brother.

"We are glad to see you again, we really missed you," were Stéphanie's opening words on my return to the dairy products section. There had been several changes in my absence. First off, the arrival of a newcomer, Samuel, 23 years old, who has bounced from job to job since he dropped out of school.

"I couldn't wait for you to get back to help me take care of the day-care," joked Stéphanie, referring to our teens. I think she was happy to see me return because I am a reliable employee. I have to admit that I am not unhappy to be back. A new manifestation of the Bentonville syndrome? The simple, hard work at Walmart is not entirely adverse. In addition to making calories melt away, there is never any work to bring home as there is at the newspaper, where my schedule is dictated by the news. But, I'd just come from a trip, was rested and in a good mood; maybe this led me to see life positively.

Antonin was transferred to reception and I inherited new responsibilities. Again! I now have to order the milk and file reports about losses. My days are starting to be more cluttered than the apartment of someone with Diogenes syndrome. At the same salary, it is better to be a carefree, testosterone-filled teen, who comes to work as though it is a summer camp, than the old guy who works full time and on whom the manager relies.

The young people nevertheless pay for their indolence. They are often lectured by the boss. A youth who takes care of the shopping carts surprised me once in the washroom while I was surreptitiously browsing my iPhone and congratulated me in a tone of complicity.

"You're starting to learn a few things … but watch out," he warned in a low tone. "I've already had two warnings. Three times and you're out!"

I was about to take my lunch break when a pack of customers surrounded me. They had been waiting ten minutes for an associate in the furniture department. A fight broke out to determine who would be served first. First come, first served. It's the rule. But who could claim that title?

"I've been waiting ten minutes," ranted one lady.

"Ten minutes, bah, I've been waiting much longer. The other day it was so long, I left the store," shot back a mustachioed man.

The floodgate of complaints was opened: "You can never find anything here"; "You want to save money so much that you don't hire staff"; and of course the age-old, "You always change everything around!" I maintained a stoic smile throughout this cathartic session.

When it was over, I left in an embarrassment of apologies from the store. Despite the magnitude of the tragedy afflicting them, I think I did them good.

In the afternoon, Marc summoned me into a small office. He closed the door and immediately asked me for the latest on my supposedly dying mother-in-law. I had forgotten all about her!

"Her condition is stable, but our farewells have been said."

In the event of a funeral, I would not be returning. My boss, damn him, was once again sympathetic.

"I have never gone through that, but it must not be easy."

His face lit up as he announced, "On a happier note, you have gotten the full-time job. Congratulations!"

This status guaranteed a minimum number of hours. But it came with yet more responsibilities: the same as a manager, but without the salary.

Did I mention that I don't mind the work in dairy products but that my salary is no joke? Judge for yourself: for nearly forty hours of work per week, you earn about $320 net. And new tasks are regularly added to an already long list: keep the temperature log updated; order milk; deal with the pallets' manage the "part-timers"; serve customers (a task that shouldn't be trivialized); change prices; and, every morning, remove and replace the six or seven pallets, one by one, which encumber the too-small fridge.

"You must be happy!" cried the store manager.

Yes indeed. Minimum salary with three times more responsibilities! Only an ingrate would complain.

BLACK FRIDAY

November 23, 2012

Today is Black Friday, so called because the day marks the time of year when retail businesses begin to accumulate profit. They move out of the red. This American tradition consists of ransacking stores the day after Thanksgiving to take advantage of the fabulous sales officially launching the holiday season. Walmart feeds this folly by offering unbelievable discounts on some items.

Dozens of customers were languishing outside the store this morning. As soon as the doors opened, they literally stampeded towards the electronics department, where the big sales were to be found. Some let off joyful yells of victory, others ran like sprinters, earning them calls to order from one of the managers.

"Sir, please, sir, we don't run," the manager scolded a tall oaf in his 50s, rushing to take advantage of a major discount on a plasma tv.

I escaped this depressing tradition "thanks" to a training course to learn to drive a propane forklift. With this driver's licence, I would be able to fetch the pallets of goods in the refrigerated trailer outside. The course took place in a windowless room. A dozen associates participated, mostly night workers who had just finished their shift. The foul odour permeating the airless room testified to their hard nocturnal labour.

The young trainer enriched his presentation with several supposedly funny videos of accidents, gleaned from YouTube. He also peppered it with off-colour jokes: "What sound does the horn in a prostitute's car make? Hoor-hoor!"

I was not a good audience for such idiocy, but the guy in front of me must have liked the show — he was sporting a sweatshirt with a witticism worthy of Alfred Jarry: "Attention, allergic to work. Warning, in case of attack, apply two weeks of vacation."

Stéphanie was convinced that I was dying to drive the lift. Appearances can be deceitful. I still have difficulty putting windshield wiper fluid in a car and the revving of a motor is about as exciting to me as fireworks are to a blind person.

I passed the propane forklift course with flying colours. To my great surprise, I had as much fun as a kid driving my yellow racing car, like the old Tonka cars of my childhood. The licence was a poisoned gift, however, because the managers of several other departments now started to ask me to transport their goods. Another new responsibility.

At the end of the day, I also discovered that this little toy did not come without risks. The forklift was on empty. Richard sent me in my car to fill two propane tanks. The safety of hauling two seventy-litre tanks of propane, rattling together in the trunk of my car, was not obvious to me. I didn't remember a training module about this. I began to regret having accepted the mission. All the more so because gas was leaking from one of the tanks. "Hey, I've never seen that before," said the young employee filling the tanks, clarifying that he didn't think it was dangerous. Very reassuring.

I spent the trip back to the store reviewing the best moments of my life. Not too bad. I have two children. My name would live on. I could already see the headlines "Journalist infiltrating Walmart dies in car explosion!" Well, it was one news item that I would not have to cover for *La Presse*! I could imagine the article without difficulty. There would be an interview with a propane specialist (yes, there are specialists for everything), who would explain that it is completely suicidal to carry two full tanks in a car; another with the employee who filled the tanks, wrestling with his conscience; and a final one with Walmart, which would refuse to comment so as not to affect the CSST investigation. An investigation the company would obviously contest.

Returning to the store in one piece, I noticed that the police were there. Not for a propane tank explosion. They were there to stop a fight between two customers.

LA VACHE QUI PLEURE (THE CRYING COW)[6]

December 5, 2012

We work too hard for miserable wages at this rotten store. I am repeating myself but it was the only thing running through my mind as I puffed and pulled heavy pallets of milk or juice. Before going to the damned trailer to get the pallets, I had to go on a quest to find the key for the garage and trailer. A quest, yes, because the few keepers of the keys — trusted managers — guard them as jealously as Frodo's ring. Each time they hand them over, they make me feel as if an extraordinary privilege were being conferred on me. All to stock their fucking yogurt pallets!

Near the end of the once more grueling day, punctuated by a

stunningly redundant repertoire of swear words, Stéphanie added a layer by asking, in a sarcastic tone,

"How old are you?"

"Um, 34."

"And you're deaf already? I called you on the intercom several times."

Fuck. As though I had been chilling my ass. I hadn't heard anything because I was running around like a chicken with its head cut off since morning, shouldering the entire job alone. Not content with heaping criticism on me, Stéphanie announced that they were giving me two new responsibilities: changing the prices when new promotions were on; and cleaning the floor of the fridge each morning. Every morning, I would have to heave out the many wobbly pallets encumbering our small fridge, one by one. Then I would clean the floor with a mop and put everything back.

And then there was Christian, who never came. In fact, the problem was not that he was late. The real problem was a billionaire company too stingy to hire more employees, squeezing the few it hired to the last drop. With the holiday frenzy, it started to affect morale. Beginning with Mélissa, who saw her hours melt away like the PQ party during elections. A question of budget, she was told.

"If it continues like this, I will have no choice but to leave. It's too bad, I like working here," sighed the young woman in dismay.

Her angry colleagues pled her cause to anyone who would listen. In their eyes, Mélissa's woes were due to the company's strategy of reducing the workforce to a bare minimum to increase profits. It seemed obvious. Part-time associates in many sections were seeing their hours cut drastically at the very moment that the holiday crush was intensifying.

Christiane, a manager fired during a company restructuring in 2014, told me in a subsequent interview that the associates were correct. Reducing staff during peak periods is common practice.

"The budgets are very … even too tight," explained Christiane. Every year, "the manager calculates [their budgetary forecasts] using the previous year's figures and must always 'adjust upwards' the percentage of revenues for the coming year. I guess that the morning meetings, where yesterday's sales figures are compared to the previous year's on the same date, are meant to remind managers of their duty to achieve performance objectives."

"Hours are cut during the peak period between November and January," Christiane explained, "because the managers have not reached the expected sales figures for the year. The department managers are putting the squeeze on. They have to make a lot of money, with as few staff as possible."

The revolt that had been brewing in the fruit and vegetable department for a few weeks was starting to spill over into the dairy section. Antonin had left and now Christian was threatening to leave. He had applied to an IGA close to his home.

"I can't stand working here any more!" he moaned all day long. He may well have arrived late today. It was not a time of celebration in the store, despite the Christmas decorations sparkling in each aisle.

Stéphanie went to Marc's office to complain about the lack of staff in our department. I discreetly approached to overhear snatches of their conversation.

"Yes, but we need someone experienced. In fact, the ideal would be a clone of Hugo!" Marc told her. Ouch. They will be very disappointed: I am preparing to leave.

Preparing to jump ship is causing me anxiety. The company's culture and its cheap positive reinforcement techniques have had the desired effect on my psychology: I feel that I am letting down the multi-billion-dollar multinational by leaving. There is a grain of truth in this feeling of guilt. Walmart will survive my departure, but my colleagues will have to work all the harder during the holiday season, because the store doesn't seem in any hurry to hire or train new people. I plan to make the announcement early next week. I feel I am going to hate the next few days.

A customer interrupted my reverie. She asked me very seriously where to find "La Vache qui pleure" (The Crying Cow) cheese.

(In front of you, Madame, right in front of you.)

THE CHRISTMAS PARTY

December 13, 2012

I am a bit put out with my *La Presse* colleagues who I feel have abandoned me to this work camp without remorse or regret. I have been here more than two months and virtually no one has deigned to come see me, go for a coffee or ask how I was doing. This is only half true. My colleague, Chantal, invited me to her birthday dinner yesterday, along with award-winning author, Dany Laferrière, who seemed to find my adventures at Walmart very amusing. Chantal and he had been in Haiti for a bookfair when the earthquake happened in 2010. Tragedy creates bonds. I am still a bit upset about the lack of inquiries from other colleagues about my new conditions of life. But, out of sight, out of mind, as they say.

An exchange of emails among *La Presse* staff alerts me to a debate raging at the newspaper. The organizer of the sumptuous Christmas party rented a room in a building that also houses a famous bar with nude dancers. Is it ethical to drink wine and eat delicious appetizers in such a place?

Meanwhile, my associate colleagues eat frozen meals every day at noon. They don't have the leisure to discuss points of conscience with the others, nor to challenge any decision whatsoever. Often, there is nothing to bite into but the bridle. Many are my mother's age, they take breaks to breathe a little, climbing the stairs to the store, their worn hands shaking slightly as they grip the railing. But I want to reassure my associate friends: if they can't make ends meet, my fellow journalists will participate in the media food drive to come to their aid.

I heard Stéphanie say again that if any more associates in her section jumped ship, it would put everyone in trouble.

But I pushed these dark thoughts aside until later, because it was time to celebrate. Today was our "Christmas Party." I am putting it in quotation marks because I am not sure the term corresponds to the reality.

The party started with "bad news." A boss announced that yesterday's profits decreased by 20 percent from the previous year. We "only" made $207,000 yesterday. "It doesn't look good for the bonus," sighed Christian. Lamenting decreased profits to minimum-wage workers takes a lot of nerve. I guess this is called working for the economy: we all tighten our belts so that profit margins can increase. Austerity is the virtue of low earners.

The break room had been redecorated for the Christmas lunch. The tables were covered in paper tablecloths, an anorexic Christmas tree had been erected and rolls of paper towels were offered to employees. Holiday CDs played on a little stereo that disappeared after the party. Boxes of chicken from a rotisserie were handed out to everyone who had ordered them two weeks ago. Most people ate in silence or played with their phones. A few older women chattered noisily. "Hey, I've been here thirteen years and it's the first time we get chicken!" one of them exclaimed before tracing out a few dance steps between the tables of the cluttered room.

A few bottles of soft drinks and house-brand cookies were also generously given to the partygoers. The bosses held a draw for a few gifts. Christian was jubilant to win a multiple-head screwdriver.

RESIGNATION

December 16, 2012

It's done, I gave in my resignation after a long night of tossing and turning in bed.

When I closed the door of the store on the dry December cold, Mélissa was already filling her meat shelves. She didn't believe me when I told her I was leaving. To her, like others, I had no reason to complain. I was one of the few whose hours had not been cut. That was true, until today. I learned on the billboard that I had been given twenty-one hours for the next two weeks, right in the middle of the holiday season.

Twenty-one hours on minimum wage is completely insufficient to support a family. Calculate it, you will see that I am not exaggerating. In any case, there was no need to convince my colleagues that

I should seize an opportunity to quit this job for a better one. Those who remain often have no other options. Mélissa is also dreaming of packing her bags. Her hours have become ridiculous. Today she worked 6:00 – 11:00 a.m.

"I heard they are hiring at Ikea. The salaries start at $16."

Stéphanie arrived a few minutes after me. I waited two long hours before telling her I was resigning. I was worried about her reaction, especially since she constantly cited me as her model employee. I brought it up in the fridge, as we were doing a little cleaning.

"I have to tell you something and I wanted you to be the first to know: I am resigning. I found something better paying. I am leaving after Boxing Day."

I initially saw sadness or maybe disappointment on her face. But Stéphanie quickly recovered her composure.

"There is a big turnover here and we can't criticize anyone for finding something better. I am happy for you!"

She never asked what the better-paying job was and never again mentioned my departure. The discussion was closed and she quickly brought me back to earth.

"Check the dates on the yogurt. Anything that is December 19 or sooner is out."

"Yes, boss!"

My shoulders freed from an immense weight, I felt light, despite my fatigue. I went up to take my break. A coffee, before announcing my departure to Caroline at Human Resources.

"Where will you work?"

"I am going to Canada Post. On call to start with."

In vain, Caroline asked me to stay until January 5. Impossible. I start the day after Boxing Day. She seemed a little disappointed, but departures happen frequently at Walmart. This wasn't the first she had seen.

"At the end of your last day, come back here to sign some documents, give back your badge, 10 percent discount card and vest."

Richard, who was replacing Marc (at the bedside of his seriously ill father), held out the possibility of a managerial career to try to keep me.

"You know guys like you can climb in this company. You could have a promotion and help start a new store."

To my huge surprise, I felt a moment of hesitation. Very brief. I was mostly flattered. Before I could even turn him down, a security guard, disguised as a customer, grabbed me by the arm. "Follow me!"

Near the door, he intercepted a giant with a child's face. A thief. He didn't resist. We escorted the young wrongdoer to the security office in the back. His theft: three pairs of small gloves and a pair of earrings. His booty must have been worth about $10. The security agent saw him put the goods in the pockets of his winter coat. In the office, he sighed at the young man, whose eyes were riveted on the floor, ashamed.

"I will give you a chance. You just turned 18. You don't want to get a criminal record and wreck your life for a few pairs of gloves? Go, but don't steal any more, not here or anywhere else," the security agent ordered him in a paternal tone.

"No, sir, thank you, sir," the young giant muttered as he left the store miserably.

LIFE GOES ON

December 17–18, 2012

Marc was the next to learn of my departure. I told him as soon as he returned to the store. He was in a somber mood. His father was in a really bad way.

"That's too bad. But I am happy for you all the same," he sighed; obviously, his mind was elsewhere.

In just a couple of minutes, he moved on to the gaping holes in the juice section. Life goes on.

After the bosses, I could officially tell my colleagues, those I was closest to. Karine, Christian, Sylvain, Léo, Liam and Samuel all had the same reaction: "Sorry to lose you, but it's normal."

They understood that I had a family to support. They were still unaware that my family lived well thanks to my salary as a journalist. I took their phone numbers so that I could tell them the truth before the story was published. Every day, I wondered how they would react.

My adventure is drawing to a close. The bosses don't ask much of me anymore. I am jumping ship, no point bothering with me. I have the same feeling with my colleagues. Karine and Mélissa were conspiring in a low voice near a counter. I approached. They stopped talking.

"No point telling you this, you are leaving us," says Karine.

Marc came to see me in my section, where I was working alone. My section was well filled, the facing almost finished. The boss was satisfied.

"If you ever change your mind, we'd like to keep you," he said, adding that he understood perfectly well why I would be tempted by a better-paying job. "We are all looking for the same thing in the end," Marc philosophized.

I slowed down after announcing my resignation. My heart was no longer in it, as they say. I am moulting; returning to my journalist self. The eternal return of the same is starting to bore me prodigiously. Yesterday at the morning meeting, a manager again cited lower profits over the previous year, putting the bonus at risk of decrease. The store nevertheless recorded revenues of $207,000. To add insult to injury, a manager asked employees to take their coats to the cloakroom BEFORE punching in. Doing the contrary would constitute a theft of time AND a loss of productivity, and thus a virtual drop in the bonus.

As I left the store, a soft snow was falling on the parking lot. Cars were criss-crossing it in search of an elusive spot. The store was overflowing. Again, and always. My days begin and end with the sound of scrapers on car windsheilds.

I haven't seen the sun for two days.

BOXING DAY

December 26, 2012

My last day was not the least of days. It was the much-dreaded Boxing Day. A big day for bargain hunters. For me, it was an emotional time of saying farewell. The end of a long imposture. The end of a long lie.

I thought about it as I parked my car, entered the store, passed Nancy, who was standing on tiptoes to put meat on the shelf, and punched in. I ran into Marc.

"Your last day!"

"Yes."

I felt a twinge. I looked at the customers — excited, impatient — they wouldn't miss me. I tried in vain to understand why people put themselves through so much annoyance and frustration the day after Christmas. To save? I understand that less-wealthy people are looking for savings, but I don't think that Wii consoles or other video games and films — by far the most looted shelves — are exactly essential.

I spent my last hours with Liam, my fellow conspirator. He spoke again of the exploitation of which he says he is a victim. He was putting up with staying in order to improve his cv.

I started my round of farewells. I said goodbye to Jimmy, who never stops complaining. I said goodbye to Nancy; this morning, she had not dared to go look at the line-up outside the store before the opening for fear of getting into an argument.

"I can't mess around, I need this job!"

I said goodbye to Vanessa; three-quarters of her family works here.

"You aren't going to spend your life here, eh, Vanessa?! Go back to school!"

"Yes, yes, don't worry."

I also said goodbye to Sylvain, mimic of singers, specialist in a virile tremolo and a fine connaisseur of B-films; thanks to whom my time here has sometimes been a lot of fun. I finally said goodbye to Mélissa. My dear Méli, my colleague from the first moment, to whom I wish all the happiness in the world.

It was time. I went to the personnel office to sign the documents. I checked off the things I had to return to the company. Vest, knife, badge, 10 percent discount card. I left it all lying on the desk. I returned to the store in a black tshirt and pants, exactly as I had arrived three months before. I looked for Marc. He had gone to eat. Danielle, another manager I had hardly spoken to before, served as witnesss. She shook my hand.

"Good luck."

I didn't see Marc.

"Please say goodbye for me."

I punched my card for the last time, climbed the stairs and, for the last time, passed the poster that stands in for the stone tablets at Walmart, "The most important person you will see today is your next customer."

I crossed the store, passing the old Portuguese men who had adapted their routine to the abnormal Boxing Day hours, and saw Fernando at the entrance for the last time. Busy amusing a lost child with his incredible mimicry, he didn't see me. The doors opened automatically in front of me. People were arguing over a cart nearby.

I would never set foot in a Walmart again.

★

EPILOGUE

I didn't write this book with the intention of shaking the walls of the Walmart temple, or even cracking its foundations. My goal was much more modest. I simply wanted to get into the shoes of an associate and give an account of this reality from the inside. I supplemented the personal journal with facts gleaned from my readings on the topic, taking a step back from my experience as a Walmart employee. It was a sociological experiment, mixed with a bit of nostalgia for me, as I had worked at a supermarket for five years to pay for my studies. I wanted, as honestly as possible, to show life at Walmart, what it means to depend on Walmart for your living.

One of the most difficult aspects of this immersion was the long deception it necessitated. For three months, people trusted me; confided thousands of frustrations in me. They believed I was part of the gang. This lie was necessary to carry out my investigation. At the beginning it was a bit of a challenge to invent a new identity. I felt quite proud when I was handed my vest and my "customer service specialist" badge. But it still felt like a tightrope. One quick Google search of my name and I was cooked. I imagine that the news of my infiltration caused a stir. This is the only regret I have, of having possibly hurt people.

Over the weeks, I also became aware of the bubble I am lucky to live in as a journalist. One day I watched my new colleagues heating yesterday's leftovers and frozen meals in the break room microwaves. That morning I had feasted at a breakfast restaurant. Poached eggs, yogurt, fruit cocktail, café au lait. The bill was $20. I left a $3 tip. For me it was nothing. But it represented more than two hours of work for an associate. My colleague, who has already spent a third of her daily salary to take her daughter by taxi to her mother's at 3:00 a.m., couldn't even dream of such a breakfast.

In these details we see an entire world separating people who may pass each other in the street, read the same papers, vote in the same elections, follow the same laws, breathe the same air. It is easy to forget. Even normal. But if we don't pay more attention to these differences, there is a real risk that these worlds will become so far apart that they will be totally alien to each other. Those who speak in the name of everyone, who generally want for nothing, would no longer speak for anyone but themselves. We would no longer share a society.

To have a world in common, you have to be able to put yourself in the other's shoes.

★

NOTES

Foreword

1. Our translation.
2. Nelson Lichtenstein and Susan Strasser, *Walmart: L'entreprise-monde, (Walmart, Company-World),* Paris, Les Prairies ordinaires, 2009, p. 20–21.
3. Gilles Biassette and Lysiane J. Baudu, *Travailler plus pour gagner moins: La menace Walmart,* Paris, Hachette, 2008, p. 8; our translation.
4. Mères avec pouvoir (Mothers with Power) and Déclic.

Chapter 1: Culture Shock

1. For example, *Boxing Day Sale Fight at Walmart in Vancouver,* 26 December 2012 <www.youtube.com/watch?v=FTh5ciW0PJA>.
2. All names of associates in the Saint-Léonard store are fictitious.
3. Olivera Perkins, "Is Walmart's Request of Associates to Help Provide Thanksgiving Dinner for Co-Workers Proof of Low Wages?" *Cleveland Plain Dealer,* November 2013 < https://www.cleveland.com/business/index.ssf/2013/11/is_walmarts_request_of_associa.html>.
4. Gilles Biassette and Lysiane J. Baudu, *Travailler plus pour gagner moins: La menace Walmart,* Paris, Hachette, 2008, p. 47; our translation.
5. Sylvia Allegretto, "The Few, the Proud, the Very Rich," *The Berkeley Blog,* 2011 <http://blogs.berkeley.edu/2011/12/05/the-few-the-proud-the-very-rich>.

Chapter 2: Hey, I Just Met You ... and This Is Crazy

1. Nelson Lichtenstein and Susan Strasser, *Walmart: L'entreprise-monde,* Paris, Les Prairies ordinaires, 2009, p. 55; our translation.
2. Former spokesperson for Quebec solidaire, a leftist political party.

Chapter 3: Between the Army and Walt Disney

1. Our translation.
2. From Walmart website in 2014.

Chapter 4: Pilgrimage to Walmartville

1. Ron Loveless and Anna Morter, *Walmart Inside Out: From Stockboy to Stockholder,* Las Vegas, Stephens Press, 2011.
2. Extract of Sam Walton's speech during the Presidential Medal of Freedom awards ceremony in 1992 (many consider this quote as the company's official creed).
3. *Ibid.*
4. Nelson Lichtenstein and Susan Strasser, *Walmart: L'entreprise-monde,* Paris, Les Prairies ordinaires, 2009, p. 20.
5. Gilles Biassette and Lysiane J. Baudu, *Travailler plus pour gagner moins: La menace Walmart,* Paris, Hachette, 2008, p. 107; our translation.
6. Lichtenstein and Strasser, *Walmart* , p. 22; our translation.
7. Sam Walton (with John Huey), *Made in America: My Story,* New York, DoubleDay, 1992, p. 8.
8. *Ibid.*
9. Lichtenstein and Strasser, *Walmart,* p. 7; our translation.
10. *Ibid.*
11. *Ibid.,* p. 8; our translation.
12. Biassette and Baudu, *Travailler plus pour gagner moins,* p. 42; our translation.
13. *Ibid.,* p. 40–41; our translation.
14. Lichtenstein and Strasser, *Walmart,* p. 7.

Chapter 6: Hold on, Hugo!

1. Literally "pure wool"; refers to people in Quebec descended from French settlers.
2. Dina Spector, "18 Facts About Walmart That Will Blow Your Mind," *Business Insider,* 15 November 2012 < www.businessinsider.com/crazy-facts-about-walmart-2012-11?op=1>.

Chapter 7:Diary of an Associate I

1. A convenience store specializing in tobacco products.
2. Carl Renaud, "Target ouvrira au moins 105 magasins (Target to open at least 105 Stores)," *Argent,* 26 May 2011 <http://argent.canoe.ca/nouvelles/affaires/target-ouvrira-au-moins-105-magasins-26052011>.
3. In French, "vous" rather than the informal "tu."

Chapter 8: Diary of an Associate II

1. Quebec reality show — the French version of *The Voice.*
2. In French, embûches (obstacles) and embauches (hires) sound very similar.

Chapter 9: Operation Sun

1. Radio-Canada, "Walmart prend de court ses employés de Jonquière (Walmart Catches Its Jonquière Employees by Surprise)," *Nouvelles*, 29 April 2005; our translation.
2. Alain Dalongeville, Charles-Antoine Bachand, Patrick Poirier, Julia Poyet and Stéphanie Demers, *Regards sur les sociétés* [*A Look at Companies*] vol. 2, Anjou, Éditions CEC, 2014.
3. Gilles Biassette and Lysiane J. Baudu, *Travailler plus pour gagner moins: La menace Walmart*, Paris, Hachette, 2008, p. 179; our translation.
4. Walmart, "Trousse d'information pour demeurer non-syndiqué à l'intention du personnel de gérance" (Wal-Mart: A Manager's Toolbox to Remaining Union Free. CONFIDENTIAL. WALMART), 1997.
5. *Ibid.*, p. 2.
6. *Ibid.*
7. *Ibid.*, p. 3.
8. *Ibid.*, p. 9.
9. *Ibid.*, p. 5.
10. *Ibid.*, p. 10.
11. *Ibid.*, p. 12.
12. *Ibid.*, p. 16.
13. *Ibid.*, p. 24.
14. Biassette and Baudu, *Travailler plus pour gagner moins*, p. 187; our translation.
15. Human Rights Watch, "Discounting Rights. Wal-Mart's Violation of US Workers' Right to Freedom of Association," May 2007, p. 2.
16. From a document given to Hugo Muenier, as with all Walmart employees, at his first meeting to begin his employment.

Chapter 10: Diary of an Associate III

1. David Barstow, "Vast Mexico Bribery Case Hushed Up by Wal-Mart after Top-Level Struggle," *New York Times*, 21 April 2012 <www.nytimes.com/2012/04/22/business/at-wal-mart-in-mexico-a-bribe-inquiry-silenced.html?pagewanted=all&_r=0>.
2. Gilles Biassette and Lysiane J. Baudu, *Travailler plus pour gagner moins: La menace Walmart*, Paris, Hachette, 2008, p. 144; our translation.
3. *Ibid.*, p. 144; our translation.
4. *Ibid.*; our translation.
5. *Ibid.*, p. 150; our translation.
6. *La Vache qui rit*, a brand of cheese, literally means The Laughing Cow.

★

ACKNOWLEDGEMENTS

This project obviously could not have materialized without my editors Mark Fortier and Alexandre Sánchez at Lux, who quickly saw the literary potential of this experience, not to mention allowing an (other) reporter to sharpen his pen at a time when journalism is dissipating into diverse formats and platforms and going through dark times. For the English version of the book: thanks to Magpie Translations for translating and to Wayne Antony and all the people at Fernwood Publishing and Marie-Ève Lamy at Lux Éditeur for bringing my experience of Walmart to English readers.

To the employees of Saint-Léonard, who played a role in this book, despite themselves, and who reminded me every day, again in spite of themselves, that I have nothing to complain about.

To my girlfriend Martine for all her work, except cleaning. To my second-floor tenants — and incidentally, parents — Micheline and Claude, who allow me to have a hectic life. To my children Victor and Simone, just for being cute. To Katia Gagnon, source of inspiration and one of the best writers on the market. To Ninon Pednault, whose talent greatly contributes to making me less of a dull old uncle. To my colleague, Chantal Guy, who passed on the email from Lux. To my bosses at *La Presse*, Jean-François Bégin and Martin Pelchat, who read, re-read and re-re-read my Walmart stuff to the point of overdose. To my friend, Martin Tremblay, for his encouragement. To Roxane Larouche, Quebec spokesperson for the United Food and Commercial Workers of Canada (UFCW), for her invaluable help. To Patrice Bergeron and

Gaétan Plourde for their journey back in time. To my colleague, Marie-Eve Fournier, and HEC Montreal Professor JoAnne Labrecque for their expertise. To Isabelle Massé so that she finally stops ignoring me. To Patrick Lagacé, whom I name-drop for no reason at all in the hope of selling three or four more books. And finally, to Sam Walton, without whom I could never have written this book.